Silver Burdett Ginn Science
# DISCOVERYWORKS

# SCIENCE NOTEBOOK

## ACTIVITIES

## UNIT PROJECTS

## INVESTIGATE FURTHER

**Silver Burdett Ginn**
PARSIPPANY, NJ    NEEDHAM, MA
Atlanta, GA    Deerfield, IL    Irving, TX    Santa Clara, CA

**CREDITS**
**Contributing artists**
Susan Simon, Deborah Pinckney

**Silver Burdett Ginn**
**A Division of Simon & Schuster**
**299 Jefferson Road, P.O. Box 480**
**Parsippany, NJ 07054-0480**

ISBN 0-382-33511-2

6 7 8 9 10 H 05 04 03 02 01 00 99 98 97

# CONTENTS

## UNIT D    MAGNETISM AND ELECTRICITY. . . 145

## UNIT E    WEATHER AND CLIMATE . . . . . . . . 201

**UNIT A**

Name_____ Date_____

# EARTH'S LAND RESOURCES

In Unit A you'll learn about natural resources and their wise use. For the Unit Project Big Event, you'll plan an exhibit of your state's natural resources. What do you think a natural resource is?

A natural resource is _____

_____

What natural resources from your state can you name? List as many as you can think of in the space below.

Name_____ Date_____

# UNIT PREVIEW

What do you know about natural resources? What would you
like to learn? List your questions on the lines below.

_____

_____

_____

_____

_____

_____

_____

_____

_____

_____

_____

*Earth's Land Resources* • Unit A

**CHAPTER PREVIEW**

Name_____ Date_____

# THE SHAPE OF THE LAND

Think about the shape of the land in the area where you live.
Think about how land looks in other places. Draw one of the
shapes that land can take.

Name_____ Date_____

Dear Journal,

Some of the different shapes of land that I have seen are . . .

_____

_____

_____

_____

_____

I think the different shapes of the land are formed by . . .

_____

_____

_____

_____

After a long period of time, I think the shapes of the land will change in this way . . .

_____

_____

_____

_____

**ACTIVITY RECORD**

Name_____ Date_____

# HILLS AND VALLEYS

## Procedure

**Write your prediction** about what will happen to the sand when you make it "rain" on top of the hill.

_____

_____

_____

**Make a drawing** in the space below that shows where the water makes a "stream," a "river," and an "ocean" in the pan. Add the labels *stream, river,* and *ocean*.

**Describe the experiments** your group will try with different-shaped hills and more than one rainmaker.

_____

_____

_____

_____

Name_____ Date_____

In the space below, **make drawings** of your observations as you experiment with different-shaped hills and more than one rainmaker.

## Analyze and Conclude

Write the answers to the questions in your book on the lines below.

1. _____

_____

_____

2. _____

_____

3. _____

_____

_____

Name_____ Date_____

# UNIT PROJECT LINK
· · · · · · · · · · · · · · · · · · · · · · · · · · · · · · ·

Make a list of scenic places in your state that you already
know about.

_____

_____

_____

_____

Use a state map to locate other scenic places in your state
that you don't already know about. List these places below.

_____

_____

_____

_____

List the scenic places in your state that you would like to
learn more about.

_____

_____

_____

_____

Share this information with your group.

Name_____ Date_____

# AT THE BEACH

## Procedure

**Record** the changes you observe in the beach as you make waves with the ruler.

_____

_____

**Write your prediction** about what will happen to the waves and the beach if you make waves that hit the jetty. Explain your prediction.

_____

_____

_____

**Record your observations** of the beach and the waves as you make waves that hit the jetty.

_____

_____

_____

## Analyze and Conclude

Write the answers to the questions in your book on the lines below.

1. _____

_____

_____

**ACTIVITY RECORD**

Name_____ Date_____

**2.** _____

_____

**3.** _____

_____

_____

**INVESTIGATE FURTHER!**

**EXPERIMENT**

Page A9

**Write a hypothesis** that explains how the direction from which the waves come might affect a beach differently.

**Describe your plan** and how it will test your hypothesis.

How do your findings agree or disagree with your hypothesis?

Name_____ Date_____

 THINK IT WRITE IT

# INVESTIGATION 1

......................................

**1.** Suppose you wanted to build a house at the shore. Would you choose to build it on a rocky shore or a sandy beach? Give reasons for your answer.

_____

_____

_____

**2.** Describe at least two land shapes that are formed by moving water.

_____

_____

_____

Draw a diagram that traces the path of a raindrop from the time it falls on land until it reaches a lake or an ocean.

Name_____ Date_____

# BLOWIN' IN THE WIND

## Procedure

**Record** the changes you observe in the surface of the sand after blowing it with the hair dryer.

_____

_____

**Write your prediction** about how the surface of the sand with sticks on it will look after the surface has been blown. Give reasons for your prediction.

_____

_____

_____

**Record** the changes you observe in the surface of the sand with sticks on it after blowing across the surface.

_____

_____

_____

## Analyze and Conclude

Write the answers to the questions in your book on the lines below.

**1.** _____

_____

_____

**ACTIVITY RECORD**

Name_____ Date_____

2. _____

_____

_____

3. _____

_____

_____

**INVESTIGATE FURTHER!**
...............
**EXPERIMENT**

Page A17

**Predict** how the plants will affect the surface of the sand when it's blown.

**Record** the changes you observe in the surface of the sand with plants in it after the surface has been blown.

**Infer** the effect that plants have on the erosion of sand in desert areas.

**ACTIVITY RECORD**

CHAPTER **1**

Name_____ Date_____

# GIGANTIC FROZEN SANDPAPER

## Procedure

**Write your prediction** about what will happen when you move the glacier over the rock.

_____

_____

_____

**Record** the changes you observe in the rock after moving the glacier over it.

_____

_____

_____

## Analyze and Conclude

Write the answers to the questions in your book on the lines below.

1. _____

_____

_____

2. _____

_____

_____

Name _____ Date _____

**INVESTIGATE FURTHER!**
· · · · · · · · · · · · · ·
**RESEARCH**

Page A19

**Record** the name of the reference book you use to learn about the effect a glacier had on Kelley's Island.

What land shapes on Kelley's Island were probably caused by glaciers?

**Infer** how a glacier formed the shape of the land on Kelley's Island.

Name_____ Date_____

 # INVESTIGATION 2

**1.** Suppose a giant snowball rolled down a hill, collecting sticks, pebbles, and soil on its way. Then warm weather arrived and melted the snowball. Compare the material left when the snowball melted with a moraine.

_____

_____

_____

_____

**2.** Describe one way that wind shapes land and one way that glaciers shape land.

_____

_____

_____

_____

Draw how moving ice could change the shape of a V-shaped valley formed by a river.

**CHAPTER WRAP-UP**

Use with page A25.

Name_____ Date_____

# THE SHAPE OF THE LAND

How does moving water shape the land?

_____

_____

_____

_____

How do wind and ice shape the land?

_____

_____

_____

_____

Look again at the land shape you drew on page 3. Infer how moving water, wind, or moving ice might have formed this land shape.

_____

_____

_____

_____

**CHAPTER WRAP-UP**

Name_____ Date_____

Think about what you learned in Chapter 1 when you answer the following questions.

**1.** Describe the most interesting thing you learned about how the land is shaped.

_____

_____

_____

_____

**2.** How does what you learned in the chapter change the way you look at the shape of the land around you?

_____

_____

_____

_____

**3.** What else would you like to learn about the shape of land and the forces that change it? What could you do to find out about it?

_____

_____

_____

_____

**CHAPTER PREVIEW**

CHAPTER 2

Name_____ Date_____

# THE IMPORTANCE OF NATURAL RESOURCES

Think about all the things in your house. Which are made of materials from Earth? Which need energy to work? Draw some of these things in this house.

**Unit A • *Earth's Land Resources***     19

**CHAPTER PREVIEW**

Use with pages A26–A27.

Name_____ Date_____

Dear Journal,

Natural resources that I know about are . . .

_____

_____

_____

_____

I use natural resources when I do these things . . .

_____

_____

_____

_____

I can conserve natural resources by doing these things . . .

_____

_____

_____

_____

Name_____ Date_____

# LITTLE ONES FROM BIG

## Procedure

**Write your prediction** about what you would see if you poured the water from the jar through the filter.

_____

_____

_____

**Record** what you observe on the filter paper with a hand lens.

_____

_____

_____

## Analyze and Conclude

Write the answer to the question in your book on the lines below.

_____

_____

_____

_____

Name_____ Date_____

# SAVING SOIL

## Procedure

**Write your prediction** about how rain might affect the soil in each pan.

_____

_____

_____

**Record your observations** of the soil in the pans when you make it "rain" over them.

_____

_____

_____

## Analyze and Conclude

Write the answers to the questions in your book on the lines below.

1. _____

_____

_____

2. _____

_____

_____

Name_____ Date_____

# UNIT PROJECT LINK
· · · · · · · · · · · · · · · · · · · · · · · · · · · · · · · · · · · · · · ·

List the natural resources that you think are important in
your community.

_____

_____

_____

_____

_____

Which natural resources would you like to focus on in the
newsletter?

_____

_____

_____

What features would you like to see in the newsletter?
Which articles would you like to write?

_____

_____

_____

Share this information with your group.

Name_____ Date_____

THINK IT
WRITE IT

# INVESTIGATION 1

**1.** Suppose your town wants a park, but the only land available is bare and full of gullies. Make a plan to convince the town leaders that the available land can be used to make the park.

_____

_____

_____

_____

_____

**2.** Explain how the processes of weathering and erosion relate to soil.

_____

_____

_____

Draw a diagram showing one way to conserve soil.

**ACTIVITY RECORD**

Name_____ Date_____

# EXPLORING MINERALS

## Procedure

Complete the chart below. Then write the names of the minerals in it. **Record your results** as you observe and test each mineral.

| Mineral | Properties | | | |
|---|---|---|---|---|
| | Hardness | Shiny | Makes a streak | Attracted to a Magnet |
| | | | | |

**ACTIVITY RECORD**

Use with pages A34–A35.

Name _____ Date _____

**Write your prediction** about the hardness of the minerals by listing the minerals from softest to hardest.

_____

_____

**Record your findings** about what materials come from the minerals you observed.

_____

_____

_____

_____

_____

## Analyze and Conclude

Write the answers to the questions in your book on the lines below.

1. _____

_____

_____

2. _____

_____

3. _____

_____

_____

**ACTIVITY RECORD**

Name_____ Date_____

# BEING POLITE ABOUT RESOURCES

## Procedure

**Write a prediction** about how many paper clips will be left at the end of the game.

_____

## Analyze and Conclude

Write the answers to the questions in your book on the lines below.

1. _____

_____

2. _____

_____

3. _____

_____

INVESTIGATE FURTHER!

TAKE ACTION

Page A37

**Make a list** of items you use that are made of metals.

What could you do to make sure that future generations will have metal resources?

Name_____ Date_____

 THINK IT WRITE IT

# INVESTIGATION 2
......................................

**1.** Pretend you have discovered a new mineral. Name the mineral and describe its properties. Then explain how the mineral can be used.

_____

_____

_____

**2.** Write a short paragraph that explains why rocks are important resources.

_____

_____

_____

_____

_____

In the space below, make a word web in which you define and show the relationships among the words *resources, renewable resources,* and *nonrenewable resources.* Include in your web at least one example of both a renewable and a nonrenewable resource and tell how the resources are used.

**ACTIVITY RECORD**

CHAPTER **2**

Name_____ Date_____

# SUN-TOASTED MARSHMALLOWS
·············································································

## Procedure

**Write your prediction** about which thermometer will show the highest temperature when the reflectors are placed in sunlight. Explain your prediction.

_____

_____

_____

**Record** the temperature from each thermometer.

_____

_____

**Write your prediction** about whether the time of day will make a difference in the temperature readings.

_____

_____

_____

**Record** the temperature readings from each thermometer at different times of the day.

_____

_____

_____

Name_____ Date_____

In the space below, **make a drawing** of the solar cooker that you design to toast a marshmallow.

**Record the results** of cooking the marshmallow in your solar cooker. How long did it take for your marshmallow to cook?

_____

_____

## Analyze and Conclude

Write the answers to the questions in your book on the lines below.

1._____

_____

_____

2._____

_____

3._____

**INVESTIGATE FURTHER**

Name_____ Date_____

INVESTIGATE
FURTHER!
EXPERIMENT

Page A45

**Draw a diagram** of your design for a solar water heater.

**Predict** how hot you can get the water in 30 minutes.

What were your results?

Name_____ Date_____

 THINK IT WRITE IT

# INVESTIGATION 3
• • • • • • • • • • • • • • • • • • • • • • • • • • • • • •

**1.** Choose one of these kinds of energy—solar energy, wind energy, or energy from inside Earth. Explain why using that kind of energy might be better than using energy from fossil fuels.

_____

_____

_____

**2.** Name the three main fossil fuels and tell why they should be conserved.

_____

_____

_____

In the space below, show the major steps in the formation of fossil fuels.

**CHAPTER WRAP-UP**

Name_____ Date _____

# THE IMPORTANCE OF NATURAL RESOURCES

Why is soil an important resource?

_____

_____

_____

_____

Why are rocks and minerals important resources?

_____

_____

_____

_____

Look back at the objects you drew in the house on page 19. Why are energy resources so important?

_____

_____

_____

_____

Name_____ Date_____

Think about what you learned in Chapter 2 when you answer the following questions.

**1.** What did you learn in this chapter that changes the way you live?

_____

_____

_____

_____

**2.** What was the most surprising thing you read about natural resources?

_____

_____

_____

_____

**3.** What else would you like to know about natural resources? What could you do to find out?

_____

_____

_____

_____

**CHAPTER PREVIEW**

Name_____ Date_____

# THE PROBLEM WITH TRASH

Think of your favorite outdoor place. Draw what it looks like.

Use with pages A52–A53.

Name_____ Date_____

Dear Journal,

My favorite outdoor place is affected by trash in these ways . . .

_____

_____

_____

_____

I think the trash got there by . . .

_____

_____

_____

_____

My thoughts about trash in the environment are . . .

_____

_____

_____

_____

**ACTIVITY RECORD**

Name_____ Date_____

# LOOKING AT TRASH

## Procedure

**Record your prediction** about what material most of the trash will be made of.

_____

In the chart below, **record** each trash item and the group to which it belongs.

| Group (Material Item Is Made Of) | Item of Trash |
|---|---|
|  |  |

**Make a bar graph** in the space below to show your data.

Name_____ Date_____

## Analyze and Conclude

Write the answers to the questions in your book on the lines below.

1. _____

2. _____

   _____

3. _____

   _____

   _____

**INVESTIGATE FURTHER!**

**EXPERIMENT**

Page A55

**Make a list** below of all the trash produced by your class in one day.

**Make a bar graph** on a piece of graph paper to show how many items from each group of trash is thrown away by your class. Keep the graph in your *Science Notebook*.

**Infer** what material in schools is thrown away in the greatest amount.

**ACTIVITY RECORD**

Name_____ Date_____

# MAKING A LANDFILL

## Procedure

**Write your prediction** about what will happen to each kind of trash after it's been buried for two weeks.

_____

_____

_____

**Record** the changes you observe in the wastes after two weeks.

| Waste | Change |
|-------|--------|
|       |        |

## Analyze and Conclude

Write the answers to the questions in your book on the lines below.

1. _____

_____

_____

Name_____ Date_____

2. _____

_____

_____

3. _____

_____

_____

**INVESTIGATE FURTHER!**

**EXPERIMENT**

Page A57

**Predict** what will happen to the trash after three months.

**Compare** your prediction to the results.

**Infer** what happens to trash in a landfill over long periods of time.

Name_____ Date_____

# INVESTIGATION 1
......................................

**1.** Imagine that you are in charge of getting rid of your town's trash. If you had to choose between burning it and burying it, which method would you use? Give reasons for your choice.

_____

_____

_____

_____

**2.** If you were to examine the contents of a town's garbage bags, what type of trash would you expect to find most of? Explain your answer.

_____

_____

_____

Make a diagram to show where trash can go.

Name_____ Date_____

# A LITTER WALK

## Procedure

**Make a list** below of the kinds of litter that you see on your litter walk.

_____

_____

_____

_____

Write the categories below that your group will use to classify the litter on your list. How many items of trash do you have from each category?

_____

_____

**Make a chart or bar graph** below to show the number of items from each trash group.

**ACTIVITY RECORD**

CHAPTER 3

Name_____ Date_____

## Analyze and Conclude

Write the answers to the questions in your book on the lines below.

1. _____

   _____

   _____

2. _____

   _____

   _____

   _____

Name_____ Date_____

# CLEAN IT UP!
..........................................

## Procedure

**Record your observations** of the oily sand after one hour.

_____

_____

_____

**Write your prediction** about which method will best clean up
the oil in the sand.

_____

_____

_____

**Describe your plan** for cleaning up the oil.

_____

_____

_____

**Record the results** as you work to remove the oil from the sand.

_____

_____

_____

Name_____ Date_____

## Analyze and Conclude

Write the answers to the questions in your book on the lines below.

1. _____

_____

_____

_____

2. _____

_____

**INVESTIGATE FURTHER!**

**RESEARCH**

Page A63

What oil spill are you going to research?

What methods were used to clean up the spill you found out about?

Has the damage to the environment been completely repaired? Explain.

Name_____ Date_____

# INVESTIGATION 2

· · · · · · · · · · · · · · · · · · · · · · · · · · · · · · · · · · · ·

**1.** Pretend that you are a detective. Look for evidence of land pollution in your community. Record your observations. Then suggest the cause and how this pollution might be prevented.

_____

_____

_____

_____

**2.** Name two ways that trash can affect available natural resources.

_____

_____

_____

In the space below, make a compare/contrast diagram that shows the relationships among *hazardous wastes, land pollution,* and *litter.*

**ACTIVITY RECORD**

CHAPTER 3

Name_____ Date_____

# RECYCLING OLD NEWS
· · · · · · · · · · · · · · · · · · · · · · · · · · · · · · · · · · · · · · ·

## Procedure

**Write your prediction** about what the new paper you are making
will be like.

_____

_____

_____

## Analyze and Conclude

Write the answers to the questions in your book on the lines below.

**1.** _____

_____

_____

_____

_____

**2.** _____

_____

_____

_____

_____

Name_____ Date_____

INVESTIGATE
FURTHER!
...............
EXPERIMENT

Page A69

What did you add to your paper pulp?

What do you plan to do with your paper when it's dry?
**Describe your plan** below.

Name_____ Date_____

# THE RETHINK LINK

## Procedure

**Make a plan** for a way to save resources.

_____

_____

_____

**Write a prediction** about how your plan to save resources will work.

_____

_____

**Record the results** of your plan to save resources.

_____

_____

## Analyze and Conclude

Write the answers to the questions in your book on the lines below.

1._____

_____

_____

2._____

_____

_____

Name_____ Date_____

# A SECOND LIFE FOR TRASH

## Procedure

**Write your prediction** about the number of places in your community there are to take items for recycling or reuse.

_____

**Record** in the chart below the information for each recycling center and store that you identify.

| Where To Recycle and Reuse | | | |
|---|---|---|---|
| Name and Address | Telephone Number | Kinds of Items Accepted | Payment Given for Items |
| | | | |

**ACTIVITY RECORD**

CHAPTER 3

Name_____ Date_____

## Analyze and Conclude

Write the answers to the questions in your book on the lines below.

1._____

_____

_____

_____

2._____

_____

3._____

_____

_____

_____

**UNIT PROJECT LINK**

Name_____ Date_____

# UNIT PROJECT LINK
· · · · · · · · · · · · · · · · · · · · · · · · · · · · · · · · ·

Identify one natural resource from your state that you
would like your group to focus on.

_____

_____

_____

_____

Where in your state is this natural resource found? How is it
obtained?

_____

_____

_____

_____

How is the natural resource used? Name some things that
are made from this natural resource.

_____

_____

_____

_____

Share this information with your group.

## INVESTIGATE FURTHER

Name_____ Date_____

**INVESTIGATE FURTHER!**
· · · · · · · · · · · · · · ·
**TAKE ACTION**

Page A77

**Describe your plan** for measuring the amount of packaging used in items brought home.

**Make a chart** to organize the data you collect.

**Describe your plan** for reducing the amount of packaging used by your family.

Name_____ Date_____

# INVESTIGATION 3
• • • • • • • • • • • • • • • • • • • • • • • • • • • • • • • •

**1.** Most people agree that reducing the amount of packaging
would help conserve natural resources and save space in land-
fills. Why is it difficult to reduce packaging?

_____

_____

_____

_____

**2.** What are four ways that you can help reduce trash? Describe
them.

_____

_____

_____

_____

Draw a diagram that shows how aluminum is recycled.

Name_____ Date_____

# THE PROBLEM WITH TRASH

What do people throw away and where does it go?

_____

_____

_____

_____

How can trash affect resources?

_____

_____

_____

_____

Think about the favorite outdoor place that you drew on page 35 and about how litter, or trash thrown on the ground, might affect it. How can you help solve the trash problem?

_____

_____

_____

_____

_____

**CHAPTER WRAP-UP**

Use with page A79.

Name_____ Date_____

Think about what you learned in Chapter 3 when you answer the following questions.

**1.** What surprised you most as you read "The Problem With Trash"?

_____

_____

_____

_____

**2.** What was the most interesting thing you learned?

_____

_____

_____

_____

**3.** Tell something else you would like to learn about the topic of trash. How could you find out about this topic?

_____

_____

_____

_____

_____

UNIT
A

Name_____ Date_____

# UNIT PROJECT WRAP-UP

Think about the natural resources that were featured in the Unit A Big Event—an exhibit of your state's natural resources. Which of your state's natural resources do you think is most important? Explain why.

_____

_____

_____

_____

Is this natural resource a renewable or a nonrenewable resource?

_____

_____

Describe several ways that you can help conserve this natural resource.

_____

_____

_____

_____

_____

**Unit A • *Earth's Land Resources***

Name_____ Date_____

# PROPERTIES OF MATTER

In Unit B you'll learn about the properties of matter. For the Unit Project Big Event, you'll set up a science museum with exhibits of matter and its properties. What do you think matter is?

Matter is _____

_____

_____

Name some things you can see that are matter.

_____

_____

_____

_____

What are some things you can't see that are matter?

_____

_____

_____

How would you describe matter to someone?

_____

_____

_____

Name_____ Date_____

# UNIT PREVIEW
......................................................

What do you know about matter and its properties? Think
about what you'd like to learn. Make a list of your ideas on
the lines below.

_____

_____

_____

_____

_____

_____

_____

_____

_____

_____

_____

Name_____ Date_____

# DESCRIBING MATTER

Choose an object and think about how massive it is and how long it is. Draw the object on the balance and next to the ruler to show its mass and length.

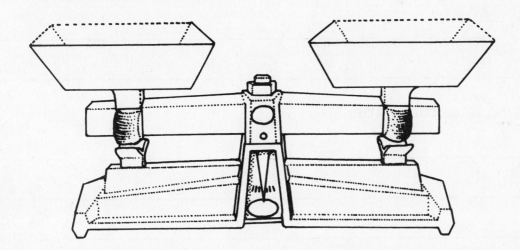

Name_____ Date_____

Dear Journal,

Some different kinds of matter that I have seen today are . . .

_____

_____

_____

_____

_____

Words that I use to describe matter are . . .

_____

_____

_____

I find out what matter is like in these ways . . .

_____

_____

_____

I can measure matter using these tools . . .

_____

_____

_____

**ACTIVITY RECORD**

Name_____ Date_____

# DESCRIBING THINGS

## Procedure

**Make a chart** in the space below in which you can **record** the name of each object you observe and its description.

| Object | Description |
|--------|-------------|
|        |             |

**Make inferences** about the properties of each object as you handle it. Write this information in your chart.

**Record the properties** you chose to classify the objects.

_____

Name_____ Date_____

## Analyze and Conclude

Write the answers to the questions in your book on the lines below.

1. _____

   _____

2. _____

   _____

3. _____

   _____

   _____

   _____

**INVESTIGATE FURTHER**

Name_____ Date_____

INVESTIGATE
FURTHER!
...............
EXPERIMENT

Page B7

Which objects from the activity "Describing Things" do you predict will float? Which objects do you predict will sink?

What were your results?

Name_____ Date_____

# SIMILAR BUT DIFFERENT
••••••••••••••••••••••••••••••••••••••••••••

## Procedure

**Rank** the numbered balls from largest to smallest.

_____

**Write your prediction** about the amount of matter in each ball by writing the number of the balls in order from heaviest to lightest.

_____

_____

After comparing how heavy the balls are, **rank** the numbered balls again from heaviest to lightest.

_____

## Analyze and Conclude

Write the answers to the questions in your book on the lines below.

1._____

_____

_____

2._____

_____

3._____

_____

Name_____ Date_____

# MOVE OVER
· · · · · · · · · · · · · · · · · · · · · · · ·

## Procedure

**Write your prediction** about where the level of the water will be
when you pour it into the jar with two marbles in it.

_____

_____

**Compare** the water level you predicted with the water level you
observe in the jar with two marbles.

_____

_____

## Analyze and Conclude

Write the answers to the questions in your book on the lines below.

1. _____

_____

_____

2. _____

_____

3. _____

_____

_____

Name_____ Date_____

# UNIT PROJECT LINK
....................................................

List several objects that can be measured in different ways.

_____

_____

_____

_____

_____

Which objects would you like to include in your Matter
Mysteries display? Explain why.

_____

_____

_____

_____

Write a question for these objects that would challenge
museum visitors to order the objects by mass or volume.

_____

_____

_____

_____

Share this information with your group.

Name_____ Date_____

# INVESTIGATION 1
......................................................

**1.** Look at this list: hammer, ice cube, mirror, rubber balloon. For each object, identify the property or properties that make the material that the object is made of useful.

_____

_____

_____

**2.** Imagine that you are going on a trip to the South Pole. Name two nonfood items you would bring with you and tell why each would be useful.

_____

_____

_____

In the space below, make a word web that shows the relationships among the words *matter, mass, volume, physical properties,* and *chemical properties*. Define each of these words in your web.

Name_____ Date_____

# A BALANCING ACT

## Procedure

**Infer** how you will know when both pans contain the same amount of matter.

_____

**Record** in the space below the objects from bag A that have the same amount of matter as the rock.

_____

**Write your prediction** about how many objects from bag B will balance the rock. Explain your prediction.

_____

**Record** the number of objects from bag B that balance the rock.

_____

## Analyze and Conclude

Write the answers to the questions in your book on the lines below.

**1.**_____

**2.**_____

_____

**3.**_____

_____

CHAPTER
1

Name_____ Date_____

# WIDER OR TALLER?

## Procedure

**Record** the model's height and arm span when you use your measuring tool.

_____

_____

**Write a prediction** about how your measurements will compare with your partner's measurements when you use the same measuring tool.

_____

_____

**Record your measurements** of height and arm span using your partner's measuring tool.

_____

_____

## Analyze and Conclude

Write the answers to the questions in your book on the lines below.

1. _____

_____

2. _____

_____

Name _____ Date _____

# How Much?

## Procedure

**Draw a diagram** in the space below that shows each container and the letter you gave it.

**Write an inference** about which container can hold the most matter. Explain.

_____

_____

_____

In the space below **write a plan** to find out how much matter each container can hold.

_____

_____

_____

**ACTIVITY RECORD**

Name_____ Date_____

**Record** which container can hold the most matter.

_____

_____

## Analyze and Conclude

Write the answers to the questions in your book on the lines below.

1._____

_____

_____

2._____

_____

_____

Name_____ Date_____

# INVESTIGATION 2
............................................

**1.** Suppose you want to move a desk into your bedroom. What properties of the desk will you have to measure?

_____

_____

_____

**2.** You want to make enough fruit punch to fill a large punch bowl. What property of the bowl do you need to measure? How would you make the measurement?

_____

_____

_____

Draw a diagram of a measuring tool and tell what it measures.

**CHAPTER WRAP-UP**

Name_____ Date _____

# DESCRIBING MATTER
·······························

How can matter be described?

_____

_____

_____

_____

How can matter be measured?

_____

_____

_____

_____

Think about the object you drew on page 61. You "measured" some of that object's physical properties. Now tell some more properties of this object.

_____

_____

_____

_____

Name_____ Date_____

Think about what you learned in Chapter 1 when you answer the following questions.

**1.** What surprised you the most as you read "Describing Matter"? Explain why.

_____

_____

_____

_____

**2.** Describe the most useful thing you learned.

_____

_____

_____

_____

**3.** What else would you like to learn about how matter is described? What could you do to find out?

_____

_____

_____

_____

Name_____ Date_____

# OBSERVING STATES OF MATTER

Think about water and how it can be a solid, a liquid, or a gas.
Complete each scene to show how the environment looks when
water is a solid, a liquid, and a gas.

| SOLID | LIQUID | GAS |
| --- | --- | --- |

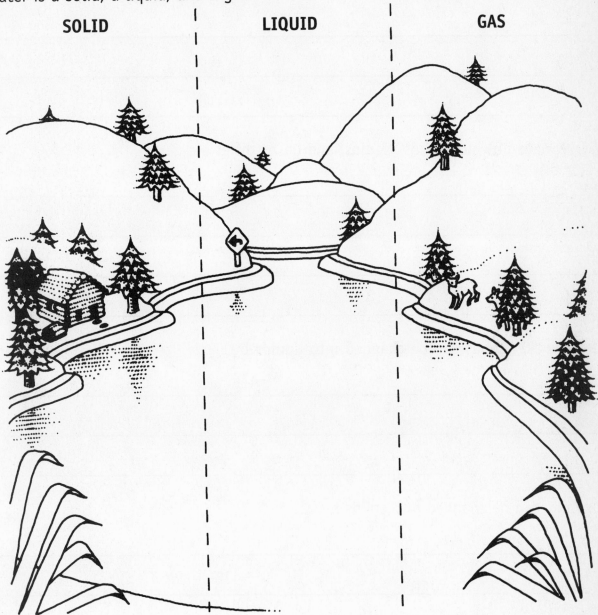

Name_____ Date_____

Dear Journal,

I know that the three states of matter are . . .

_____

I think that matter is made up of these things . . .

_____

_____

_____

Some ways in which solids, liquids, and gases differ are . . .

_____

_____

_____

_____

I know that solids can be changed into liquids by . . .

_____

_____

_____

Liquids can be changed into solids by . . .

_____

_____

_____

**ACTIVITY RECORD**

CHAPTER 2

Name_____ Date_____

# STATES OF MATTER
........................................

## Procedure

**Record your descriptions** of objects A through E.

A _____

B _____

C _____

D _____

E _____

**Record** the changes you observe in the objects as you shake them in the containers.

A _____

B _____

C _____

D _____

E _____

**Record** any changes you observe in the shape of the water in each container.

_____

_____

Name_____ Date_____

**Record your observations** of an inflated balloon when you press
on it and when you stop pressing on it.

_____

_____

**Write your prediction** about what will happen to the air inside
the balloon when you untie it.

_____

_____

**Record your observations** about what happens to the air inside
the balloon when you remove the twist tie.

_____

_____

## Analyze and Conclude

Write the answers to the questions in your book on the lines below.

1. _____

_____

2. _____

_____

3. _____

_____

**UNIT B**

Name_____ Date_____

# UNIT PROJECT LINK
·············································

List as many materials as you can think of in the space
below that you can present in a form or state different from
that in which they are usually found.

_____

_____

_____

_____

Which three materials from your list above would you like
your group to display? List these materials below and
explain why you think they should be displayed.

_____

_____

_____

_____

Think about what you would like the signs for the states of
matter display to look like. What information would you like
your signs to give? Write your ideas below.

_____

_____

_____

Share this information with your group.

Name _____ Date _____

# INVISIBLE MATTER

## Procedure

Record your **observations** of odors in the large plastic jar.

_____

_____

Record your **observations** of odors in the bottle of vanilla extract.

_____

_____

Record your **observations** of odors in the large plastic jar after it sat over the bottle of vanilla extract for about one minute.

_____

_____

In the space below, **make a drawing** to show how the odor of vanilla got into the large plastic jar.

**ACTIVITY RECORD**

Name _____ Date _____

## Analyze and Conclude

Write the answers to the questions in your book on the lines below.

1. _____

_____

_____

2. _____

_____

_____

_____

Name_____ Date _____

# INVESTIGATION 1
••••••••••••••••••••••••••••••••••••••••

**1.** Name the three states of matter. Give a brief description of
each state.

_____

_____

_____

**2.** Suppose you had a piece of iron and a drop of water. If you
kept dividing each substance into smaller and smaller pieces,
what would the smallest piece of each substance be like?

_____

_____

_____

Diagram below the arrangement of particles in a solid, a liquid, and a gas.

**ACTIVITY RECORD**

Name_____ Date_____

# FROM STATE TO STATE

## Procedure

**Record** how your hand feels and how the ice changes as you hold the ice in your hand.

_____

_____

**Record** in the chart below the changes you observe in the ice at both spots.

| Time (in minutes) | Changes Observed in the Ice | |
| --- | --- | --- |
| | Sunny Spot | Shady Spot |
| 0 | | |
| 1 | | |
| 3 | | |
| 5 | | |
| 7 | | |
| 9 | | |
| 11 | | |
| 13 | | |
| 15 | | |

Name _____ Date _____

# Analyze and Conclude

Write the answers to the questions in your book on the lines below.

**1.** _____

_____

_____

**2.** _____

_____

_____

CHAPTER 2

Name_____ Date_____

# LIQUID FROM THIN AIR

## Procedure

**Record your observations** of the liquid that forms on the outside of the container. Tell what color this liquid is.

_____

_____

_____

## Analyze and Conclude

Write the answers to the questions in your book on the lines below.

1. _____

_____

_____

2. _____

_____

_____

3. _____

_____

_____

Name_____ Date_____

# INVESTIGATION 2

**1.** What must be done to matter in order to make it change state?

_____

_____

_____

**2.** Using what you know about changes of state, explain why water is not used as the coolant in a refrigerator instead of HFC.

_____

_____

_____

_____

Draw a diagram showing how the energy from heat affects the particles in a solid, causing the solid to become a liquid.

**CHAPTER WRAP-UP**

Name_____ Date_____

# OBSERVING STATES OF MATTER

What is matter like?

_____

_____

_____

_____

_____

Can matter change state? Explain.

_____

_____

_____

Look back at the three forms of water that you drew on page 77.
Infer how the environment caused the water to be in a certain state.

_____

_____

_____

_____

_____

Name_____ Date_____

Think about what you learned in Chapter 2 when you answer the following questions.

**1.** What interested you the most while reading this chapter?

_____

_____

_____

_____

**2.** What was the most difficult thing to understand? What could you do to help yourself understand it better?

_____

_____

_____

_____

**3.** How have the things you learned in this chapter changed the way you look at the different kinds of matter around you?

_____

_____

_____

_____

**CHAPTER PREVIEW**

Name_____ Date_____

# CAUSING CHANGES IN MATTER

• • • • • • • • • • • • • • • • • • • • • • • • • • • • • • • • • • • • • • • • • • •

Think about something you ate for dinner last night. Draw how the food looked before it was prepared and how it looked when it was ready to eat.

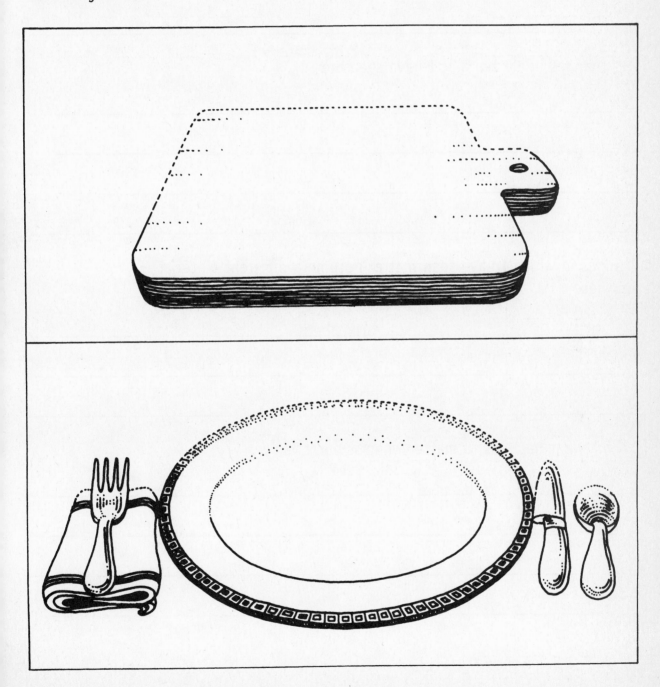

Use with pages B44–B45.

Name_____ Date_____

Dear Journal,

Kinds of matter in which I have seen changes are these . . .

_____

_____

_____

The changes in matter that I have seen are . . .

_____

_____

_____

_____

Changes in which I have seen matter become a different material
are these . . .

_____

_____

_____

I think what happens to matter when it burns is . . .

_____

_____

_____

_____

**ACTIVITY RECORD**

CHAPTER 3

Name_____ Date_____

# GO WITH THE FLOW

## Procedure

**Describe** how the liquid flowed when it was poured into cup A.

_____

_____

**Write your prediction** about which cup, A or B, will have more liquid in it.

_____

_____

**Describe** how the liquid flowed when it was poured into cup B.

_____

_____

**Record your observations** as you **compare** the amount of liquid in each cup.

_____

_____

## Analyze and Conclude

Write the answers to the questions in your book on the lines below.

**1.** _____

**ACTIVITY RECORD**

Use with pages B46–B47.

Name_____ Date_____

2. _____

_____

3. _____

_____

4. _____

_____

_____

**UNIT PROJECT LINK**

Name_____ Date_____

# UNIT PROJECT LINK
..............................................

With your group, divide up the Matter Mysteries and list
those that you would like to work on in the space below.

_____

_____

_____

_____

_____

_____

Write the answer or explanation for each Matter Mystery
that you listed above.

_____

_____

_____

_____

_____

_____

_____

_____

Share this information with your group.

Name_____ Date_____

# DIFFERENT LOOK, SAME STUFF

## Procedure

**Record your observations** of the paper before and after you change it.

Before: _____

_____

After: _____

_____

**Record your observations** of the modeling clay before and after you change it.

Before: _____

_____

After: _____

_____

**Record your observations** of the paper clip before and after you change it.

Before: _____

_____

After: _____

_____

**ACTIVITY RECORD**

Name_____ Date_____

**Record the mass** of the piece of chalk and the paper towel.

_____

_____

**Record the mass** of the ground chalk and paper towel.

_____

_____

## Analyze and Conclude

Write the answers to the questions in your book on the lines below.

1._____

_____

_____

2._____

_____

_____

3._____

_____

_____

_____

Name_____ Date_____

# ALL MIXED UP

## Procedure

**Make a chart** in the space below like the one in your book and list the items mixed together in the jars. Then **record your observations** of the appearance of the mixtures.

**Record your hypotheses** for ways to separate each mixture into its different parts.

_____

_____

_____

**Record the method** in the chart you used to separate each mixture.

**ACTIVITY RECORD**

Name_____ Date_____

## Analyze and Conclude

Write the answers to the questions in your book on the lines below.

1. _____

_____

_____

_____

2. _____

_____

_____

_____

Name_____ Date_____

 # INVESTIGATION 1

....................................................

**1.** When sugar dissolves in water, the sugar disappears. Why is this a physical change? Give examples of three other physical changes.

_____

_____

_____

**2.** Imagine you had a liquid mixture of three different substances. Each substance changes to a solid at a different temperature. How could you use this information to separate the mixture?

_____

_____

_____

Explain the relationships among the words *mixture, solution,* and *substance*.

Name_____ Date_____

# DIFFERENT LOOK, DIFFERENT STUFF

## Procedure

**Record your observations** as you add vinegar to baking soda.

_____

_____

_____

**Record your observations** of liquids *A* and *B* before and after you pour them into a jar.

_____

_____

_____

**Record your observations** of the two pieces of steel wool after they were left overnight.

_____

_____

_____

## Analyze and Conclude

Write the answers to the questions in your book on the lines below.

1. _____

_____

_____

Name_____ Date_____

**2.** _____

_____

**3.** _____

_____

_____

INVESTIGATE
FURTHER!
...................
EXPERIMENT

Page B60

**Record** the changes you observe in the steel
wool coated with oil after it was left overnight
with water under a jar.

**Compare the results** of this experiment with those of the original activity
on pages B56 and B57.

Explain any differences in these results.

Name_____ Date _____

# INVESTIGATION 2

**1.** How is the burning of paper like the rusting of iron? How are
the two changes different?

_____

_____

_____

**2.** First you sharpen a pencil. Then you throw the pencil shavings
in the fireplace and burn them. Describe the different ways
the wood changes.

_____

_____

_____

Make a diagram that shows the chemical reaction between iron, water, and oxygen
to form rust, or iron oxide.

**CHAPTER WRAP-UP**

Name_____ Date_____

# CAUSING CHANGES IN MATTER
..................................................................

What are physical changes?

_____

_____

_____

_____

What are chemical changes?

_____

_____

_____

_____

Think back on the food that you drew on page 91. When this food
was prepared to eat, was it changed chemically or physically?
Explain.

_____

_____

_____

_____

Name_____ Date_____

Think about what you learned in Chapter 3 when you answer the following questions.

**1.** What was the most surprising thing you learned while reading "Causing Changes in Matter"?

_____

_____

_____

_____

**2.** What did you learn that helped explain something that you have always wondered about?

_____

_____

_____

_____

**3.** What else would you like to know about causing changes in matter? Tell how you would find out.

_____

_____

_____

_____

Name_____ Date_____

# UNIT PROJECT WRAP-UP

Think about the Matter Mystery displays in the Science Museum you helped set up. Which Matter Mystery did you like best? Explain why.

_____

_____

_____

_____

Explain what made your favorite Matter Mystery a mystery.

_____

_____

_____

_____

Tell what kind of matter you pretended to be at the Science Museum. How did you "act it out"?

_____

_____

_____

_____

_____

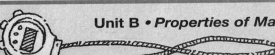

**UNIT C**

Name_____ Date_____

# ANIMALS
. . . . . . . . . . . . . . . . . .

In Unit C you'll learn about animals and how they are adapted to meet their needs. What do you think animals need to survive? List these needs below.

_____

_____

_____

What are some features of animals that help them meet their needs? List them below.

_____

_____

_____

_____

You'll also learn in this unit how different kinds of animals are classified. For the Unit Project Big Event, you'll go on a safari to identify animals, using field guides that you create. How do you think animals can be classified?

_____

_____

_____

Name_____ Date_____

# UNIT PREVIEW
• • • • • • • • • • • • • • • • • • • • • • • • • • • • • • • • •

There are probably many things you already know about animals. Think about what animals need to survive. What questions do you have? List your questions on the lines below.

_____

_____

_____

_____

_____

_____

_____

_____

_____

_____

**CHAPTER PREVIEW**

Name_____ Date_____

# ANIMALS MEET THEIR NEEDS

Pretend that you're a scientist searching for new kinds of animals in the rain forest. Draw a picture of the animal you discover.

Name_____ Date_____

Dear Journal,

The animal that I discovered in the rain forest is a . . .

_____

_____

Some basic needs of this animal are . . .

_____

_____

_____

The characteristics of this animal are . . .

_____

_____

_____

The animal may respond to its environment in these ways . . .

_____

_____

_____

_____

Name_____ Date_____

# NEEDS IN COMMON

## Procedure

In the chart below, **record** the names of the animals pictured in your book on pages C6 and C7. **Record your inference** in the chart about what need each pictured animal is trying to meet.

| Animal | Need |
|--------|------|
|        |      |

## Analyze and Conclude

Write the answers to the questions in your book on the lines below.

1. _____

_____

_____

2. _____

_____

_____

_____

Name_____ Date_____

# UNIT PROJECT LINK
......................................................

List as many animals as you can that live in your area.

_____

_____

_____

_____

_____

_____

_____

_____

Which animals listed above would you like to include in
your field guide? Make a check mark by the name of each of
these animals.

What information about these animals do you think should
be included in your field guide? Explain.

_____

_____

_____

_____

Share this information with your group.

**INVESTIGATION CLOSE**

Name_____ Date_____

# INVESTIGATION 1

······················································

**1.** Baby birds have just hatched in a nest outside your window. What basic needs do the young birds have?

_____

_____

_____

**2.** Write about an imaginary animal. Describe the type of environment in which it lives. Explain how it meets each of its basic needs. You might include drawings to help your explanations.

_____

_____

_____

_____

_____

Make a word web around the word *environment*. Include the different things in an environment that help animals meet their basic needs.

Name_____ Date_____

# FEATHER FEATS

## Procedure

**Make a drawing** in the space below showing the structure of a wing or tail feather.

**Record your observations** of the barbs on the wing or tail feather that you pull apart.

_____

_____

**Record your observations** as you pull the wing or tail feather through your fingers.

_____

_____

**Make a drawing** in the space below showing the structure of a down feather.

**Record your observations** as you pull the down feather through your fingers.

_____

**ACTIVITY RECORD**

Name_____ Date_____

**Record your observations** as you wave both feathers through the air.

_____

_____

## Analyze and Conclude

Write the answers to the questions in your book on the lines below.

1. _____

_____

_____

_____

2. _____

_____

INVESTIGATE FURTHER!
·················
**RESEARCH**

Page C15

How does the body covering you chose to research help the animal meet its basic needs?

List the sources you used for your research.

Name_____ Date_____

# COLOR ME, COLOR MY WORLD

. . . . . . . . . . . . . . . . . . . . . . . . . . . . . . . . . . . . . . . . . . . . . . . . . . . . .

## Procedure

**Write your prediction** of which color "insect" will be hardest to find when you place the pipe cleaners on the green cloth.

_____

**Record your data** in the chart below for each time you pick up the pipe cleaners.

| Trial | Number of Pipe Cleaners | | | |
|-------|------|------|-------|--------|
|       | Red  | Blue | Green | Yellow |
| 1     |      |      |       |        |
| 2     |      |      |       |        |

## Analyze and Conclude

Write the answers to the questions in your book on the lines below.

**1.**_____

_____

_____

**2.**_____

_____

_____

**INVESTIGATE FURTHER**

Name_____ Date_____

INVESTIGATE
FURTHER!
· · · · · · · · · · · ·
EXPERIMENT

Page C17

**Write your plan** to test what color of insect will be the hardest to see when the grass is yellow in the winter.

**Predict** which color of pipe cleaner will be the hardest to see.

**Make a chart** in the space below. **Record your results** for each time you pick up the pipe cleaners.

Name_____ Date_____

# INVESTIGATION 2

**1.** Write a description of your favorite animal. Describe different body parts, such as teeth, claws, a tail, scales, and feathers. Explain how each part helps your favorite animal survive.

_____

_____

_____

_____

**2.** A bat hangs upside down and flutters its wings. How does fluttering its wings help a bat meet a certain need?

_____

_____

_____

For each animal listed below, name one body part and tell how that part helps the animal meet its needs.

Brown Bear _____

_____

Emperor Penguin _____

_____

Pocket Gopher _____

_____

**ACTIVITY RECORD**

CHAPTER 1

Name_____ Date_____

# TAP, TAP, TAP

## Procedure

**Make a list** of the different behaviors you observe in the goldfish.

_____

_____

_____

_____

**Write your prediction** about how the behavior of the goldfish
might change if you try to attract them by making a sound.

_____

_____

_____

**Record your observations** of the goldfish as you tap on the wall
of the fish tank.

_____

_____

**Record your observations** of the goldfish as you tap on the wall
of the fish tank at the same time food is being added.

_____

_____

_____

Name_____ Date_____

**Record your observations** each day as you tap on the fish tank and feed the fish for two weeks.

_____

_____

_____

_____

_____

_____

_____

**Record your observations** of the goldfish as you tap on the fish tank, but do not give them food.

_____

_____

## Analyze and Conclude

Write the answers to the questions in your book on the lines below.

**1.**_____

_____

_____

**2.**_____

_____

_____

Name_____ Date_____

# UNIT PROJECT LINK

Think about the animals that you are including in your field guide. List some adaptations of each animal that help it survive. Tell how each adaptation helps the animal survive.

_____

_____

_____

_____

What kinds of behaviors help these animals to survive? List them below.

_____

_____

_____

_____

Think about some interesting ways you could add this information to your field guide. Write your ideas below.

_____

_____

_____

Share this information with your group.

Name_____ Date_____

# INVESTIGATION 3

••••••••••••••••••••••••••••••••••

**1.** A dog lies down and rolls over at the command of its owner. What kind of behaviors are these? Explain your answer.

_____

_____

_____

**2.** List three different kinds of animals. For each animal, describe one behavior that helps it meet a basic need.

_____

_____

_____

_____

Draw a diagram showing how honeybees tell the other bees at the hive where flowers with nectar are.

**CHAPTER WRAP-UP**

Name_____ Date_____

# ANIMALS MEET THEIR NEEDS
.....................................................................

What basic needs do animals share?

_____

_____

_____

Think back to the animal you drew on page 111. How do body
parts help this animal meet its needs?

_____

_____

_____

_____

_____

_____

How do behaviors help animals meet their needs?

_____

_____

_____

_____

_____

Name_____ Date_____

Think about what you learned in Chapter 1 when you answer the following questions.

**1.** What was the most interesting thing you learned as you read "Animals Meet Their Needs"?

_____

_____

_____

_____

**2.** What did you learn in this chapter that helps explain something that you have always wondered about?

_____

_____

_____

_____

**3.** What else would you like to learn about animal adaptations and how these adaptations help animals to survive? Tell how you could find out about it.

_____

_____

_____

_____

_____

**CHAPTER PREVIEW**

Name_____ Date_____

# ALL KINDS OF ANIMALS
• • • • • • • • • • • • • • • • • • • • • • • • • • • • • • • • • • • • •

Think of your favorite animal. Draw what it looks like. Complete
the picture to show the animal's environment.

CHAPTER **2**

**CHAPTER PREVIEW**

Use with pages C32–C33.

Name_____ Date_____

Dear Journal,

I think the animal I drew on page 127 can be classified as . . .

_____

_____

Some other groups of animals that I know are . . .

_____

_____

_____

Two groups in which I think all animals can be classified are . . .

_____

_____

The main difference between these two groups is . . .

_____

_____

_____

**128**    *Animals* • **Unit C**

**ACTIVITY RECORD**

Name_____ Date_____

# STUDYING BACKBONES

## Procedure

**Write your inference** about the size and shape of the bones in your backbone.

_____

_____

_____

In the space below, **make a drawing** that shows what you think your backbone looks like.

## Analyze and Conclude

Write the answer to the question in your book on the lines below.

_____

_____

_____

Name_____ Date_____

# ANIMALS ARE DIFFERENT
..............................................................

## Procedure

**Record your observations** of the ways in which the animals you're studying are alike and different.

_____

_____

_____

In the chart below, **record your observations** of the characteristics for each animal. Add more characteristics to the chart if you need to.

| Characteristics | Animal 1 | Animal 2 | Animal 3 |
|---|---|---|---|
| How It Moves | | | |
| Type of Body Covering | | | |
| Number of Legs/Description | | | |
| Number of Eyes | | | |
| Number of Ears | | | |
| Where It Might Live | | | |

**ACTIVITY RECORD**

Name_____ Date_____

**Record your observations** in the chart as you study each animal with a hand lens. Also **record your inference** in the chart of where each animal might live.

## Analyze and Conclude

Write the answers to the questions in your book on the lines below.

1. _____

   _____

   _____

2. _____

   _____

   _____

   _____

3. _____

   _____

   _____

Name_____ Date_____

# UNIT PROJECT LINK
••••••••••••••••••••••••••••••••••••••

List some different ways in which you could classify the animals that will be in your field guide.

_____

_____

_____

_____

Think about how you would like to organize the animal descriptions in your field guide. Write your ideas below.

_____

_____

_____

_____

What are some ways that you can make your field guide easy to use? Write your ideas about how a reader could find information quickly in your field guide.

_____

_____

_____

_____

Share this information with your group.

Name_____ Date _____

  # INVESTIGATION 1
··········································

**1.** An organism has no structures for moving from place to place. It makes its own food, and it reproduces by seeds. In what kingdom would you place this organism? Explain your answer.

_____

_____

_____

**2.** As you pet a dog along its back, you feel hard knobs under its skin. What are you feeling? Based on this feature, into what group of animals would you classify the dog? Explain your answer.

_____

_____

_____

Diagram with a word web the relationship among the words *animal, invertebrate, vertebrate, backbone, exoskeleton,* and *vertebra.* Give examples of vertebrates and invertebrates.

**ACTIVITY RECORD**

Use with pages C44–C45.

Name_____ Date_____

# COLD FISH

## Procedure

In the chart below, **record your measurements** of the water temperature in the goldfish jar. Then **record the number** of breaths that the goldfish takes in one minute.

|  | Water Temperature | Breathing Rate |
|---|---|---|
| First Reading |  |  |
| Two minutes after ice cubes were added |  |  |

**Write your prediction** about how the number of breaths in one minute will change if ice cubes are added to the water.

_____

In the chart **record the temperature** of the water in the goldfish jar two minutes after adding the ice. Then **record the number** of breaths the goldfish takes in one minute.

## Analyze and Conclude

Write the answers to the questions in your book on the lines below.

1. _____

   _____

2. _____

   _____

**INVESTIGATE FURTHER**

Name_____ Date_____

**INVESTIGATE
FURTHER!**
∙∙∙∙∙∙∙∙∙∙∙∙∙∙∙∙
**EXPERIMENT**

Page C45

**Predict** what will happen to the breathing rate of the goldfish when warm water is added to the goldfish jar. Explain your prediction.

**Record your observations** after adding warm water to the goldfish jar.

Water Temperature

Number of Breaths in One Minute

**Compare** your results with your prediction and with your results in the earlier activity. How do they differ?

Name_____ Date_____

# UNIT PROJECT LINK

How would you like to present the facts in your field guide to local animals? Explain why you chose this way to publish your field guide.

_____

_____

_____

_____

_____

Think about a plan to publish your field guide. Write your plan below.

_____

_____

_____

_____

_____

Look at the tasks described in your plan to publish the field guide. Which tasks would you like to do? Explain why.

_____

_____

_____

Share this information with your group.

**INVESTIGATION CLOSE**

Name_____ Date_____

# INVESTIGATION 2
······················································

**1.** Name the five groups of vertebrates. List the characteristics that are special to each group.

_____

_____

_____

_____

_____

**2.** A salmon, a penguin, and a whale can all swim. In what other ways are these three animals alike? How are they different?

_____

_____

_____

In the space below, diagram the stages in the development of a frog.

Name_____ Date_____

# WORMING THEIR WAY HOME

## Procedure

**Write your prediction** about which numbered section in the box the worm will move toward.

_____

_____

In the chart below, **record your observations** of the worm's location in the box each minute for ten minutes.

| Time (in minutes) | Location |
|---|---|
| 1 | |
| 2 | |
| 3 | |
| 4 | |
| 5 | |
| 6 | |
| 7 | |
| 8 | |
| 9 | |
| 10 | |

**ACTIVITY RECORD**

Name_____ Date_____

**Record your observations** of how the earthworm uses its body parts to move.

_____

_____

## Analyze and Conclude

Write the answers to the questions in your book on the lines below.

1. _____

_____

2. _____

_____

3. _____

_____

INVESTIGATE FURTHER!
............................
**RESEARCH**

Page C55

Explain how worms are able to turn trash into compost. What kinds of trash can worms recycle?

List the names of the sources you used for your research.

Chapter 2

Name_____ Date_____

# INVESTIGATION 3

**1.** Name eight groups of invertebrates. List the characteristics that are special to each group.

_____

_____

_____

_____

_____

_____

_____

_____

**2.** Insects have been called the most successful group of animals. What are some characteristics of insects that have helped them to live so successfully on Earth?

_____

_____

Draw a picture of your favorite invertebrate and show the environment in which it lives.

**CHAPTER WRAP-UP**

Name_____ Date_____

# ALL KINDS OF ANIMALS
......................................................

How can living things be classified?

_____

_____

_____

What are the five groups of vertebrates? How do they differ?

_____

_____

_____

_____

_____

How do the groups of invertebrates differ?

_____

_____

_____

_____

_____

_____

_____

_____

**CHAPTER WRAP-UP**

Use with page C63.

Name_____ Date_____

Think about what you learned in Chapter 2 when you answer the following questions.

**1.** How do you look at animals differently after reading this chapter? Explain.

_____

_____

_____

_____

**2.** What surprised you the most as you read this chapter? Explain why.

_____

_____

_____

_____

**3.** What else would you like to learn about how living things are classified? How could you find out more about it?

_____

_____

_____

_____

UNIT
C

Name_____ Date_____

# UNIT PROJECT WRAP-UP
· · · · · · · · · · · · · · · · · · · · · · · · · · · · · · · · · · · · · · · · · · ·

Think about the Field Guide to Local Animals that you
helped publish. What did you like best about your field
guide? Explain.

_____

_____

_____

Describe the field guide that your group borrowed on
Animal Safari Day. How was that field guide similar to or
different from your field guide?

_____

_____

_____

Where did you go on your field trip on Animal Safari Day?

_____

_____

Were you able to identify all of the animals that you observed
on your field trip? List below the animals that you identified.
If you couldn't identify some animals, explain why.

_____

_____

_____

Name_____ Date_____

# MAGNETISM AND ELECTRICITY

In Unit D you'll learn about magnetism and electricity. You'll apply what you learn by inventing devices that use either magnetism or electricity for the Unit Project Big Event—The Inventor's Fair. Whether you realize it or not, you use electricity and magnetism every day. Can you think of ways that you use magnetism? List them below.

_____

_____

_____

_____

List some ways that you use electricity.

_____

_____

_____

_____

Think about toys or games you have played with that use magnetism or electricity. List these toys in the space below.

_____

_____

_____

_____

Name_____ Date_____

# UNIT PREVIEW

Consider what you know about magnetism and electricity. What else would you like to learn? Make a list of questions on the lines below.

_____

_____

_____

_____

_____

_____

_____

_____

_____

_____

Name_____ Date_____

# MAGNETISM

The crane is holding a very large magnet. Think about what kinds of objects would stick to the magnet. Add these objects to the picture.

Name_____ Date_____

Dear Journal,

I think that a magnet is this . . .

_____

_____

_____

Magnets don't attract objects made of these materials . . .

_____

_____

_____

Some properties of magnets are . . .

_____

_____

_____

I think I could make a magnet by doing these things . . .

_____

_____

_____

_____

Name_____ Date_____

# MAKE A MAGNET

## Procedure

**Record your predictions** in the chart about which objects in your collection will stick to a magnet. **Record your observations** as you move the magnet close to each object.

**Record your predictions** below about whether a nail will attract any objects in your collection. **Record your observations** as you move the nail close to each object.

In the chart below, **record your predictions** about whether the stroked nail will attract any objects in your collection. **Record your observations** as you test each object.

| Object | Attracted To Magnet | | Attracted To Nail | | Attracted to Stroked Nail | |
|---|---|---|---|---|---|---|
| | Prediction | Actual | Prediction | Actual | Predicted | Actual |
| | | | | | | |

## Analyze and Conclude

Write the answers to the questions in your book on the lines below.

1. _____

_____

Name_____ Date_____

**2.** _____

_____

**3.** _____

_____

_____

**4.** _____

_____

_____

INVESTIGATE FURTHER!

EXPERIMENT

Page D7

**Predict** whether the number of times a nail is stroked with a magnet will affect the strength of the magnetized nail.

**Make a chart** to collect data as you test how many paper clips a magnetized nail can pick up. **Record your results** in your chart.

**Infer** how the number of strokes with a magnet affects the strength of a magnetized nail.

**ACTIVITY RECORD**

CHAPTER 1

Name_____ Date_____

# A MAGNET'S ENDS

## Procedure

**Record** the different ways you can arrange the ends of the two magnets.

_____

_____

_____

_____

**Write your prediction** about what will happen to the magnets for each arrangement.

_____

_____

_____

_____

**Record your observations** as you test each arrangement of magnets.

_____

_____

_____

_____

_____

_____

Name_____ Date_____

**Record your inference** about which end of the unknown magnet, _X_ or _Y_, is really _N_ and which is really _S_. Explain.

_____

_____

_____

**Record** whether your inference was correct after removing the tape from the unknown magnet.

_____

## Analyze and Conclude

Write the answers to the questions in your book on the lines below.

**1.**_____

_____

_____

**2.**_____

_____

_____

Name_____ Date_____

# UNIT PROJECT LINK

What kinds of materials will allow the force of a magnet to act through them? List these materials below.

_____

_____

List some objects that are attracted to magnets.

_____

_____

Think about how you could use these materials, along with a magnet, to create a magic trick. Write your ideas below.

_____

_____

_____

_____

Choose one of your ideas and list the materials you would need to build a model of it.

_____

_____

_____

_____

Share this information with your group.

Name_____ Date_____

# PULLING THROUGH

## Procedure

In the chart below, **record your predictions** about whether the magnet can attract the paper clip through the different materials.

| Force of Magnet Through Materials | | |
|---|---|---|
| Material | Prediction | Result |
| | | |

**Describe your plan** for testing whether the magnet's force can act through different materials.

_____

_____

_____

_____

**ACTIVITY RECORD**

Name_____ Date_____

Did your plan work? If not, tell how you can change it.

_____

_____

_____

_____

**Record your observations** in the chart as you test each material.

## Analyze and Conclude

Write the answers to the questions in your book on the lines below.

1. _____

_____

_____

_____

2. _____

_____

_____

_____

Name_____ Date_____

# INVESTIGATION 1
..............................................

**1.** Suppose a rock sample from Mars is brought to Earth. Pieces of the rock can be picked up by a magnet. What metal may be present in the rock?

_____

_____

**2.** Two doughnut-shaped magnets are placed on a pencil. One of the magnets floats above the other one. What makes this happen?

_____

_____

_____

_____

Make a word web about magnets. Include information about types of magnets and the properties of magnets.

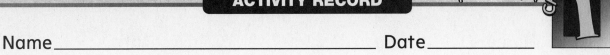

**ACTIVITY RECORD**

CHAPTER 1

Name_____ Date_____

# GETTING DIRECTIONS

## Procedure

**Record your observations** of what happens when you float the foam ball with the magnetized needle.

_____

_____

**Write your prediction** about what will happen when you move a bar magnet near the bowl.

_____

_____

**Record your observations** as you move the bar magnet near the bowl.

_____

_____

**Record your observations** as you move the bowl in a circle, a quarter turn at a time.

_____

## Analyze and Conclude

Write the answers to the questions in your book on the lines below.

**1.** _____

_____

Name_____ Date_____

2. _____

_____

3. _____

_____

_____

**INVESTIGATE FURTHER!**
.....................
**RESEARCH**

Page D17

What are magnetic domains?

**Diagram** the magnetic domains in a magnet.

**Record** the names of the sources you used for your research.

**ACTIVITY RECORD**

Name_____ Date_____

# PICTURE A MAGNET'S FORCE

## Procedure

In the space below, **draw** the pattern of iron filings on the cardboard over the bar magnet.

**Draw your prediction** of the pattern that will form when iron filings are sprinkled over the horseshoe magnet.

Name_____ Date_____

**Draw** the pattern of iron filings that you observe on the card-board over the horseshoe magnet.

## Analyze and Conclude

Write the answers to the questions in your book on the lines below.

1. _____

_____

_____

2. _____

_____

_____

**INVESTIGATE FURTHER**

Name_____ Date_____

INVESTIGATE FURTHER!
· · · · · · · · · · · · · · ·
EXPERIMENT

Page D20

What magnets will you use to make pictures of magnetic fields?

**Predict** how the lines of force will look on the magnets you chose. **Draw diagrams** of your predictions in the space below.

**Record your observations** of what you see when you brush away the rusted filings from the cardboard.

Name_____ Date_____

# INVESTIGATION 2

**1.** When a circular magnet is dipped into a pile of paper clips, about the same number of clips stick to the top as to the bottom. What does this tell you about the magnetic field of that magnet?

_____

_____

_____

**2.** How could you make a compass with a nail, a string, a plastic jar with a lid, and some tape?

_____

_____

_____

_____

Draw a diagram showing the magnetic lines of force around Earth.

**CHAPTER WRAP-UP**

Name_____ Date_____

# MAGNETISM
..............................

What are magnets? Name the two kinds of magnets.

_____

_____

_____

_____

What are magnetic force fields?

_____

_____

_____

_____

Look at the objects you drew on page 147. Would you change
any of these objects now that you know more about magnetism?
Explain.

_____

_____

_____

_____

Name_____ Date_____

Think about what you learned in Chapter 1 when you answer the following questions.

**1.** What did you learn while reading this chapter that was completely new to you?

_____

_____

_____

_____

**2.** What idea did you find to be the most difficult to understand? What could you do to help yourself understand it better?

_____

_____

_____

_____

**3.** Tell something else you would like to learn about magnetism. How could you find out about this?

_____

_____

_____

_____

_____

Name_____ Date_____

# ELECTRICAL ENERGY
. . . . . . . . . . . . . . . . . . . . . . . . . . . . . . . . . .

Look at the electric circuit. Think about an object (other than
wire) that you could connect to the circuit so that the bulb
lights up. Draw the object to complete the circuit.

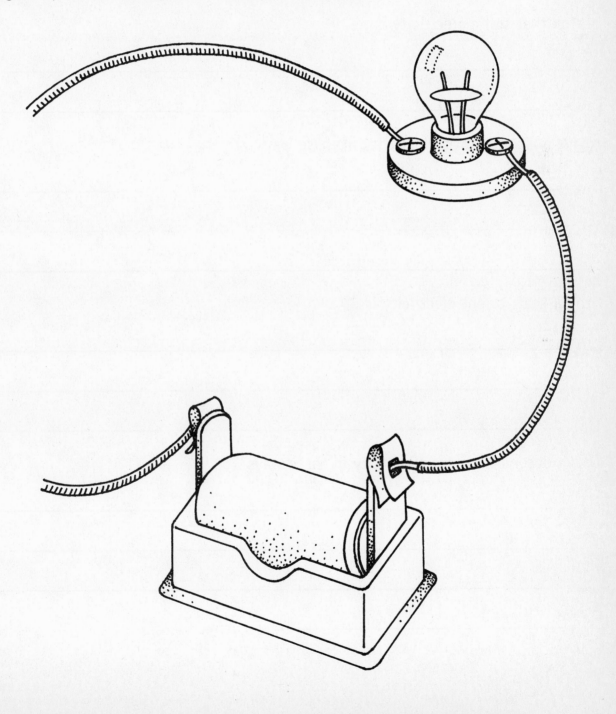

Name_____ Date_____

Dear Journal,

I know that electricity is . . .

_____

_____

I think that static electricity is . . .

_____

_____

I have observed static electricity in these ways . . .

_____

_____

_____

I think that current electricity is . . .

_____

_____

_____

I have observed current electricity in these ways . . .

_____

_____

_____

_____

**ACTIVITY RECORD**

CHAPTER **2**

Name_____ Date_____

# CHARGE!

## Procedure

**Record your observations** as you hold the two balloons about 10 cm apart.

_____

_____

**Write your prediction** about what will happen after you rub both the balloons with a wool cloth.

_____

_____

**Record your observations** as you hold the two balloons rubbed with wool near each other.

_____

_____

**Write your prediction** about what will happen after you rub the two balloons with plastic wrap.

_____

_____

**Record your observations** as you hold the two balloons rubbed with plastic wrap near each other.

_____

_____

**Write your prediction** about what will happen when a balloon rubbed with wool is brought near a balloon rubbed with plastic wrap.

_____

_____

**ACTIVITY RECORD**

Name_____ Date_____

**Record your observations** as you bring a balloon rubbed with wool near a balloon rubbed with plastic wrap.

_____

_____

## Analyze and Conclude

Write the answers to the questions in your book on the lines below.

1._____

_____

_____

_____

2._____

_____

3._____

_____

_____

4._____

_____

_____

_____

_____

Name_____ Date_____

**INVESTIGATE FURTHER!**

**EXPERIMENT**

Page D29

**Predict** how a charged balloon will affect objects that are not charged.

**Record your observations** after holding a charged balloon near cereal and near a wall.

**Infer** how a charged balloon affects uncharged objects.

**INVESTIGATE FURTHER!**

**RESEARCH**

Page D33

What experiment did Franklin perform to prove that lightning is a kind of electricity?

How do lightning rods work?

**Record** the names of the sources you used for your research.

Name_____ Date_____

# INVESTIGATION 1

................................................

**1.** How might you use a balloon with a negative charge to find out whether the charge on another balloon is positive or negative?

_____

_____

_____

**2.** Imagine you've just come inside on a cold, dry day. As you pull off your sweater, it sticks to your shirt and then you hear a crackling sound. What causes these effects?

_____

_____

_____

_____

Diagram the charges in a cloud, a tree, and the ground when lightning strikes.

**ACTIVITY RECORD**

CHAPTER **2**

Name_____ Date_____

# ON OR OFF?

. . . . . . . . . . . . . . . . . . . . . . . .

## Procedure

**Record your hypotheses** about different ways you can connect some of the parts to make the bulb light.

_____

_____

_____

In the space below, **draw** each arrangement of parts you try to make the bulb light. Circle the ones that work.

**Write your prediction** about how you can connect the switch to your circuit so that you can use it to turn the bulb on and off.

_____

_____

_____

Name_____ Date_____

**Make a drawing** that shows how the parts are connected when the switch works.

## Analyze and Conclude

Write the answers to the questions in your book on the lines below.

**1.** _____

_____

_____

**2.** _____

_____

INVESTIGATE
FURTHER!
· · · · · · · · · · · · ·
RESEARCH

Page D37

List some different kinds of switches.

Explain how these switches work.

What resources did you use to find out about switches?

**ACTIVITY RECORD**

CHAPTER 2

Name_____ Date_____

# STOP OR GO?

## Procedure

**Write your prediction** about what will happen when you touch the free ends of the wires together.

_____

_____

**Record your observations** when you touch the free ends of the wires together.

_____

_____

**Record your inference** about whether the wires in the circuit are conductors. Explain your inference.

_____

_____

_____

_____

In the chart on page 174, **record your predictions** about whether each material is a conductor or an insulator. Then **record your results** after testing each material.

Name_____ Date_____

| Conductor or Insulator | | |
| Object or Material | Prediction | Result |
| plastic straw | | |
| penny | | |
| toothpick | | |
| paper clip | | |
| rubber band | | |
| cardboard | | |
| aluminum | | |

## Analyze and Conclude

Write the answers to the questions in your book on the lines below.

1._____
_____

2._____
_____
_____

3._____
_____
_____

UNIT
D

**UNIT PROJECT LINK**

Name_____ Date_____

# UNIT PROJECT LINK
· · · · · · · · · · · · · · · · · · · · · · · · · · · · · · · · · · · · ·

Think about the questions you would like to ask on your quiz board. What question format would you like to use? Explain.

_____

_____

Write some questions and their answers in the space below.

_____

_____

_____

_____

_____

_____

Think about how the quiz board will work. Diagram how dry cells, wires, switches, and light bulbs should be arranged so that someone will know when they have answered a question correctly.

Share this information with your group.

Name_____ Date_____

# INVESTIGATION 2

. . . . . . . . . . . . . . . . . . . . . . . . . . . . . . . . . . . .

**1.** A dry cell, a light bulb, and some wires are connected in a circuit, and the bulb lights. Which part of the circuit is the source of electrical energy? Is the circuit open or closed?

_____

_____

_____

**2.** In one activity you made a switch. Would the switch work if you used aluminum foil instead of a paper clip? Explain your answer.

_____

_____

_____

Draw a diagram of an open circuit.

**ACTIVITY RECORD**

CHAPTER 2

Name_____ Date_____

# ONE TYPE OF CIRCUIT
..........................................................

## Procedure

**Draw your prediction** of the arrangement of materials that will make both bulbs light.

**Draw a diagram** of the complete circuit in which both bulbs light.

**ACTIVITY RECORD**

Name_____ Date_____

**Write your prediction** about what will happen if you take one bulb out of its holder.

_____

_____

**Record your observations** as you take one bulb out of its holder.

_____

_____

## Analyze and Conclude

Write the answers to the questions in your book on the lines below.

**1.**

**2.** _____

_____

**3.** _____

_____

_____

## INVESTIGATE FURTHER

Name_____ Date_____

In the space below, **draw a diagram** showing how you would connect another dry cell in the series circuit you constructed in the activity on pages D44–D45.

**Predict** the effect of a second dry cell in the circuit.

**Record your observations** of the effect of the second dry cell in the circuit.

Name_____ Date_____

# ANOTHER TYPE OF CIRCUIT

## Procedure

**Draw a diagram** showing your plan to connect the two bulbs, the four wires, and the dry cell.

**Record your observations** as you change the connections in your circuit to make both bulbs light.

_____

_____

**Draw a diagram** of your complete circuit in which both bulbs light.

**Write your prediction** about what will happen if you take one bulb out of its holder.

_____

_____

**ACTIVITY RECORD**

Name_____ Date_____

**Record your observations** as you take one bulb out of its holder.

_____

## Analyze and Conclude

Write the answers to the questions in your book on the lines below.

**1.**

**2.** _____

_____

INVESTIGATE FURTHER!
• • • • • • • • • • • • • •
TAKE ACTION

Page D49

How many incandescent bulbs are you using in your home?

Which fixtures or appliances with incandescent bulbs can use fluorescent bulbs?

How much money can your family save by replacing incandescent bulbs with fluorescent bulbs?

Name_____ Date_____

# INVESTIGATION 3
. . . . . . . . . . . . . . . . . . . . . . . . . . . . . . . . . . .

**1.** Explain why you can open a series circuit, but not a parallel circuit, by removing one bulb.

_____

_____

_____

_____

**2.** Suppose you want to make a parallel circuit with two light bulbs, a dry cell, and two switches. Draw the way you would connect the parts so that each switch can turn off one bulb at a time.

Why is a fluorescent bulb better for the environment than an incandescent bulb?

_____

_____

_____

Name_____ Date_____

# ELECTRICAL ENERGY

••••••••••••••••••••••••••••••••••••••••••

**What is** static electricity? How does it work?

_____

_____

_____

**What is** current electricity? Explain the difference between a conductor and an insulator.

_____

_____

_____

**What are** two kinds of electric circuits and how do they differ?

_____

_____

_____

**What kind** of circuit did you draw on page 165? Explain.

_____

_____

_____

**CHAPTER WRAP-UP**

Name_____ Date_____

Think about what you learned in Chapter 2 when you answer the following questions.

**1.** What was the most interesting thing you learned as you read "Electrical Energy"?

_____

_____

_____

_____

**2.** Tell something you learned that you can put to practical use in your life.

_____

_____

_____

_____

**3.** What was the most difficult idea to understand? What can you do to help yourself understand it better?

_____

_____

_____

_____

_____

Name_____ Date _____

# ELECTRICITY AT WORK

Think about the things you know about that need electricity to work. Now invent a machine, appliance, or other object that uses electricity. Diagram your invention and describe what it does.

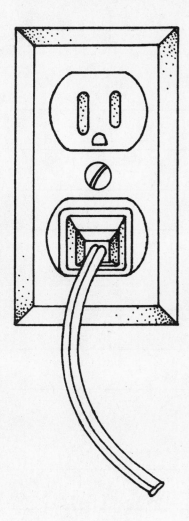

Name_____ Date_____

Dear Journal,

I think that an electric current can be made in these ways . . .

_____

_____

_____

I use electricity in these ways . . .

_____

_____

_____

_____

I think an electromagnet is . . .

_____

_____

_____

When I am using electricity, I follow these safety rules . . .

_____

_____

_____

_____

**ACTIVITY RECORD**

Name_____ Date_____

# DETECT A CURRENT

## Procedure

**Write your prediction** about what will happen when you connect the current detector to a dry cell.

_____

_____

_____

**Record your observations** when you connect the current detector to the dry cell.

_____

_____

_____

## Analyze and Conclude

Write the answers to the questions in your book on the lines below.

**1.** _____

_____

_____

**2.** _____

_____

_____

Name_____ Date_____

# A MAGNETIC SOURCE
· · · · · · · · · · · · · · · · · · · · · · · · · · · · · · · · · · · · ·

## Procedure

**Write your prediction** about how the coil of wire will affect the current detector.

_____

_____

**Write your plan** for testing the effect of the coil on the detector.

_____

_____

_____

**Record your observations** as you test the effect of the coil on the detector.

_____

_____

**Record your observations** as you move the bar magnet inside the coil of wire.

_____

_____

**Record your observations** as you hold the magnet still and quickly move the coil of wire back and forth.

_____

_____

**ACTIVITY RECORD**

CHAPTER 3

Name_____ Date_____

## Analyze and Conclude

Write the answers to the questions in your book on the lines below.

1. _____

_____

_____

_____

_____

2. _____

_____

_____

Name_____ Date_____

# A FRUITY SOURCE

## Procedure

**Write your prediction** about what will happen when you connect
the current detector to the copper strip.

_____

_____

**Record your observations** as you connect the free end of the
current detector to the copper strip.

_____

_____

## Analyze and Conclude

Write the answers to the questions in your book on the lines below.

**1.** _____

_____

_____

_____

**2.** _____

_____

**3.** _____

_____

Name_____ Date_____

INVESTIGATE FURTHER!
.................
EXPERIMENT
Page D59

What other parts will you need to make an electric cell from paper towels soaked in salt water, a penny, and a nickel?

**Draw a diagram** in the space below of the electric cell that you plan to set up.

**Record your observations** after you set up your electric cell and circuit.

Name_____ Date_____

# UNIT PROJECT LINK

Think about a device that you could build that would run on solar cells. What will this device do? List as many ideas as you can.

_____

_____

Which device do you think would be the best one to design and build? Explain.

_____

_____

How will this device work?

_____

_____

Draw a picture of what you think the device you chose should look like.

Share this information with your group.

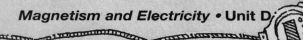

**INVESTIGATION CLOSE**

Name_____ Date_____

# INVESTIGATION 1

................................

**1.** What energy change takes place in a generator? in a battery? in a solar cell?

_____

_____

_____

**2.** Certain electric devices in the home, such as cordless tele-phones and video games, have small transformers that plug into the wall. What do the transformers do?

_____

_____

_____

Draw a diagram showing how electricity from power plants gets to your home.

Name_____ Date_____

# MAKE IT MOVE
..............................................

## Procedure

**Write your prediction** about how the nail wrapped in wire will affect the paper clips.

_____

**Record your observations** as you test how the nail wrapped in wire affects paper clips.

_____

_____

**Write your prediction** about how the nail wrapped in wire and connected to a dry cell will affect the paper clips.

_____

**Record your observations** as you test how the nail wrapped in wire and connected to a dry cell affects the paper clips.

_____

**Write your prediction** about how the nail wrapped in more wire and connected to a dry cell will affect the paper clips.

_____

**Record your observations** as you test how the nail wrapped in more wire and connected to a dry cell affects the paper clips.

_____

_____

**ACTIVITY RECORD**

Name _____ Date _____

## Analyze and Conclude

Write the answers to the questions in your book on the lines below.

1. _____

_____

2. _____

_____

_____

3. _____

_____

**INVESTIGATE FURTHER!**

**RESEARCH**

Page D69

Who made the first electromagnet?

How are permanent magnets and electromagnets used in motors?

What sources did you use for your research?

Name_____ Date _____

# INVESTIGATION 2
......................................

**1.** What devices can change different kinds of energy into electricity?

_____

_____

_____

_____

**2.** How would you explain to a group of first-graders why radios used in the bathroom should be battery-powered?

_____

_____

_____

Diagram the components of an electromagnet.

**CHAPTER WRAP-UP**

Name_____ Date_____

# ELECTRICITY AT WORK

What are some sources of electric current and how do they work?

_____

_____

_____

_____

How is electricity useful?

_____

_____

_____

_____

_____

How can you be safe around electricity?

_____

_____

_____

_____

_____

Name_____ Date_____

Think about what you learned in Chapter 3 when you answer the following questions.

**1.** What was the most interesting thing you learned about while reading this chapter?

_____

_____

_____

_____

**2.** What surprised you the most while reading this chapter?

_____

_____

_____

_____

**3.** What topic would you like to review so that you better understand it? Describe how you would review the topic.

_____

_____

_____

_____

_____

Name_____ Date_____

# UNIT PROJECT WRAP-UP

Think about the devices your group designed for the
Inventor's Fair. Which device did you like the best? Explain.

_____

_____

_____

_____

Did all of your devices work the way that you wanted them
to work? How could you have improved your devices?

_____

_____

_____

_____

What was your favorite device at the fair? How did it work?

_____

_____

_____

_____

**UNIT E**

Name_____ Date_____

# WEATHER AND CLIMATE

In Unit E you'll learn about weather and what causes it. For the Unit Project Big Event you'll give weather forecasts like the ones you've seen on TV. You'll prepare your weather forecasts from data that you collect from different instruments in your weather station. Think about weather forecasts you've seen on TV. What kinds of data does the weather forecaster use to predict the weather?

_____

_____

_____

List as many parts of a TV weather report as you can.

_____

_____

_____

_____

You'll also study seasons and climate in this unit. Think about the change of seasons in your area. How does weather change with the seasons?

_____

_____

_____

_____

Name_____ Date_____

# UNIT PREVIEW

Consider what you already know about weather. What questions do you have about how weather forecasters predict the weather? Write your questions on the lines below.

_____

_____

_____

_____

_____

_____

_____

_____

_____

_____

_____

Name_____ Date_____

# THE AIR AROUND US

Think about a windy day. Draw as many things as you can think of to show how wind affects things.

Name_____ Date_____

Dear Journal,

When I think about air, I think of these things . . .

_____

_____

_____

_____

Air is made up of . . .

_____

_____

_____

Earth's atmosphere has this structure . . .

_____

_____

_____

_____

Wind is caused by . . .

_____

_____

_____

CHAPTER 1

Name_____ Date_____

# AN EMPTY CUP

## Procedure

**Write your prediction** about what will happen when you push a cup down over a floating peanut until the cup touches the bottom of a bowl.

_____

_____

**Draw a picture** below to show your prediction.

**Record your observations** as you push the cup down over the peanut in the bowl of water.

_____

_____

**Record your observations** as you push the cup with a hole in it over the peanut in the bowl of water.

_____

_____

Name_____ Date_____

## Analyze and Conclude

Write the answers to the questions in your book on the lines below.

1. _____

_____

_____

_____

2. _____

_____

_____

_____

_____

3. _____

_____

_____

**INVESTIGATE FURTHER**

INVESTIGATE FURTHER!
••••••••••••••••••••••
EXPERIMENT

Page E7

Name_____ Date_____

**Record** the changes you observe in the water level of the bowl as your partner blows air into the water.

**Infer** what's causing a change in the water level.

**Predict** what will happen if your partner stops blowing air into the water. Explain.

Name_____ Date_____

# AN OCEAN OF AIR

## Procedure

**Record your observations** as you strike the end of the wooden slat.

_____

_____

_____

**Record your observations** as you strike the wooden slat with a newspaper on its other end.

_____

_____

_____

**Write your prediction** about what will happen when you strike the slat with half the newspaper on it.

_____

_____

_____

**Record your observations** as you strike the slat with half the newspaper on it.

_____

_____

_____

**ACTIVITY RECORD**

CHAPTER **1**

Name_____ Date_____

## Analyze and Conclude

Write the answers to the questions in your book on the lines below.

1. _____

_____

_____

2. _____

_____

_____

3. _____

_____

_____

**INVESTIGATE FURTHER!**
· · · · · · · · · · · · ·
**EXPERIMENT**

Page E9

**Record your observations** of the blown-up balloon as you press on it in different places.

**Hypothesize** what causes the balloon to have the shape it does.

How could you test your hypothesis?

Name_____ Date_____

# INVESTIGATION 1
· · · · · · · · · · · · · · · · · · · · · · · · · · · · · · ·

**1.** What is air made of? How is air like other forms of matter?

_____

_____

_____

**2.** Could there be life on Earth without the greenhouse effect?
Express your ideas about what might happen if Earth lost its
atmosphere.

_____

_____

_____

_____

Diagram the layers of Earth's atmosphere. Show how the particles
that make up air are distributed throughout the layers.

**ACTIVITY RECORD**

Name_____ Date_____

# WARMING THE AIR

## Procedure

**Record** in the chart below the air temperature you measured over the grassy area.

| Type of Surface | Temperature (°C) |
|---|---|
|  |  |
|  |  |
|  |  |

**Write your prediction** about how the air temperature over other surfaces will vary.

_____

_____

**Record** in the chart above the air temperature over two other surfaces.

## Analyze and Conclude

Write the answers to the questions in your book on the lines below.

1._____

_____

2._____

_____

Name_____ Date_____

# UNIT PROJECT LINK

In the space below, draw a diagram of the instrument you will be using to record air temperature.

Think about your results from the activity Warming the Air. Where would be a good place to mount the thermometer so that it measures air temperature accurately? Explain.

_____

_____

_____

At what time of the day do you think air temperature will be highest? lowest?

_____

_____

Share this information with your group.

**ACTIVITY RECORD**

Name_____ Date_____

# MAKING AN AIR SCALE
∙∙∙∙∙∙∙∙∙∙∙∙∙∙∙∙∙∙∙∙∙∙∙∙∙∙∙∙∙∙∙∙∙∙∙∙∙∙∙∙∙∙∙∙∙∙

## Procedure

**Write your prediction** about what will happen to the bags when the lamp is turned on.

_____

**Record** in the chart the air temperature inside both bags before turning on the lamp.

| Lamp | Temperature (°C) | |
|------|------------------|--------------|
| | Bag above lamp | Other bag |
| Off | | |
| On | | |

**Record your observations** after turning on the lamp.

_____

**Record** in the chart the air temperature inside both bags after the lamp is on.

## Analyze and Conclude

Write the answers to the questions in your book on the lines below.

**1.** _____

**2.** _____

_____

_____

_____

Name_____ Date _____

# INVESTIGATION 2
·············································

**1.** Suppose that you attach a thermometer to the wall near the ceiling of your classroom and attach another thermometer to the wall just a few centimeters above the floor. What temperature difference would you expect to find? Why?

_____

_____

_____

**2.** What does uneven heating of Earth's surface have to do with air movement?

_____

_____

_____

Draw a diagram showing how to make a hot-air balloon rise higher in the sky.

**CHAPTER WRAP-UP**

Name_____ Date _____

# THE AIR AROUND US

What is air?

_____

_____

_____

_____

Why does air move?

_____

_____

_____

_____

Look at the picture you drew on page 203. Describe what the weather is like in it.

_____

_____

_____

_____

Name_____ Date_____

Think about what you learned in Chapter 1 when you answer the following questions.

**1.** What was the most interesting thing you learned?

_____

_____

_____

_____

_____

**2.** What surprised you the most as you read the chapter?

_____

_____

_____

_____

_____

**3.** What else would you like to learn about the subject of air?
Tell how you could find out about this.

_____

_____

_____

_____

_____

**CHAPTER PREVIEW**

Name_____ Date _____

# OBSERVING WEATHER

How do you know that it's going to rain? Draw what it looks like.

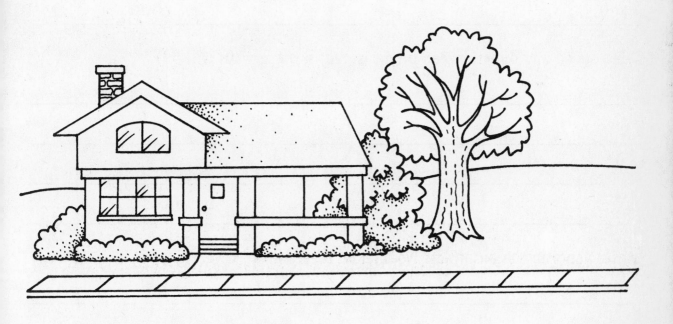

CHAPTER 2

Name_____ Date_____

Dear Journal,

I have observed these kinds of changes in the weather . . .

_____

_____

_____

_____

Air pressure affects weather in this way . . .

_____

_____

_____

_____

Wind speed and direction can be measured in these ways . . .

_____

_____

_____

_____

Water vapor in the air affects weather in these ways . . .

_____

_____

_____

_____

Name_____ Date_____

# IT'S A PRESSING PROBLEM
· · · · · · · · · · · · · · · · · · · · · · · · · · · · · · · · · · · · · · · · · ·

## Procedure

**Write your prediction** about how the plastic bottle will change when it's in hot water and then cold water. Explain your prediction.

_____

_____

_____

_____

**Record your observations** of the bottle when you remove it from the tub of hot water.

_____

_____

**Record your observations** of the bottle when you remove it from the tub of ice water.

_____

_____

## Analyze and Conclude

Write the answers to the questions in your book on the lines below.

**1.** _____

_____

_____

Name_____ Date_____

2. _____

_____

3. _____

_____

_____

_____

_____

**INVESTIGATE FURTHER!**

**EXPERIMENT**

Page E27

**Hypothesize** what will happen if you empty the hot water from the plastic bottle and quickly screw on the cap.

**Record your observations** as you empty the hot water from the bottle and quickly screw the cap back on tightly.

**Compare your results** with the results from the activity on pages E26 and E27. **Explain your observations.**

**ACTIVITY RECORD**

CHAPTER 2

Name_____ Date_____

# MEASURING AIR PRESSURE

## Procedure

In the chart below, **record** the air pressure and the weather conditions for one week.

| Date | Air Pressure Reading | Weather Conditions |
|------|---------------------|--------------------|
|      |                     |                    |
|      |                     |                    |
|      |                     |                    |
|      |                     |                    |
|      |                     |                    |

## Analyze and Conclude

Write the answers to the questions in your book on the lines below.

1. _____

_____

_____

2. _____

_____

3. _____

_____

Name_____ Date_____

# UNIT PROJECT LINK

In the space below, draw a diagram of the barometer that you chose for the class weather station.

Tell why you chose this barometer.

_____

_____

_____

Where should the barometer be located in the weather station? Explain.

_____

_____

_____

Share this information with your group.

Name_____ Date_____

# INVESTIGATION 1

......................................

**1.** You're visiting one of the tall buildings of the World Trade Center in New York City. You have a barometer with you. As you ride the elevator to the 107th floor, you notice the barometer reading goes down. Explain what happened and why.

_____

_____

_____

**2.** What is air pressure and how is it measured?

_____

_____

_____

Diagram the arrangement of air particles in a high-pressure area and in a low-pressure area. Tell which area has warm air and which has cool.

Name_____ Date_____

# A WINDY DAY

## Procedure

**Record your inference** about the direction from which the wind is blowing by observing flags or leaves moving in the wind.

_____

**Record** the wind direction you observe using the wind vane.

_____

**Observe and record** in the chart the wind direction and other weather conditions for one week.

| Date/Time | Wind Direction | Weather Conditions |
|-----------|----------------|--------------------|
|           |                |                    |

## Analyze and Conclude

Write the answers to the questions in your book on the lines below.

1. _____

_____

2. _____

_____

**UNIT PROJECT LINK**

Name_____ Date_____

# UNIT PROJECT LINK
..................................................

Draw a diagram of the wind vane that you chose for the
weather station.

Explain why you chose this wind vane.

_____

_____

_____

Where do you think the wind vane should be located in the
weather station? Explain.

_____

_____

_____

Share this information with your group.

Name_____ Date_____

# HOW FAST THE WIND BLOWS

## Procedure

**Record your hypothesis** about how an anemometer is used to measure wind speed. Explain your hypothesis.

_____

_____

_____

_____

In the chart below, **record** the wind speed and weather conditions for one week.

| Date | Time | Spins in 1 min | Weather Conditions |
|------|------|----------------|--------------------|
|      |      |                |                    |

**ACTIVITY RECORD**

Name_____ Date_____

## Analyze and Conclude

Write the answers to the questions in your book on the lines below.

1. _____

_____

_____

_____

2. _____

_____

_____

Name_____ Date_____

# UNIT PROJECT LINK

Draw a diagram below of the anemometer that you chose for the weather station.

Explain why you chose this anemometer.

_____

_____

_____

Where do you think the anemometer should be located in the weather station? Explain.

_____

_____

_____

Share this information with your group.

Name_____ Date_____

# INVESTIGATION 2
·······································

**1.** Most people would agree that wind turbines offer benefits as an energy source for producing electricity. Identify two problems in using wind turbines as a source of energy.

_____

_____

_____

**2.** How can you determine wind speed and wind direction?

_____

_____

_____

_____

Complete the word web about wind. Use the following words:
*windsock, wind vane, Beaufort scale, anemometer.*

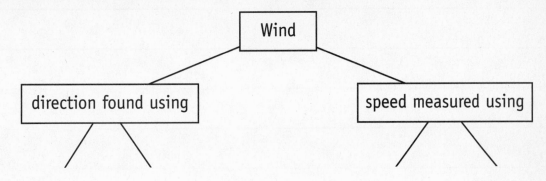

Name_____ Date_____

# MAKE A RAIN GAUGE

## Procedure

**Record** in the chart the amount of rainfall every day for one month.

| Date | Amount of Rainfall | Date | Amount of Rainfall |
|------|--------------------|------|--------------------|
|      |                    |      |                    |

## Analyze and Conclude

Write the answers to the questions in your book on the lines below.

1._____

_____

2._____

_____

3._____

_____

_____

Name_____ Date_____

# UNIT PROJECT LINK
..................................................

Draw a diagram below of the rain gauge that you chose for
the weather station.

Why did you choose this rain gauge?

_____

_____

_____

Where do you think the rain gauge should be located in the
weather station? Explain.

_____

_____

_____

Share this information with your group.

Name_____ Date_____

# INVESTIGATION 3
• • • • • • • • • • • • • • • • • • • • • • • • • • • • • • • •

**1.** Imagine that it's a cold winter day. You are outside, talking with a friend. Why can you see your breath as you talk?

_____

_____

_____

**2.** Describe the role of water vapor in weather.

_____

_____

_____

Draw four kinds of precipitation.

**CHAPTER WRAP-UP**

Name_____ Date_____

# OBSERVING WEATHER
..............................................

What is air pressure?

_____

_____

_____

_____

How can you find wind speed and direction?

_____

_____

_____

_____

How does water in the air affect weather?

_____

_____

_____

_____

**CHAPTER WRAP-UP**

Name_____ Date_____

Think about what you learned in Chapter 2 when you answer the following questions.

**1.** What was the most interesting thing you learned?

_____

_____

_____

_____

**2.** What did you learn that helped explain something you have always wondered about?

_____

_____

_____

_____

**3.** What else would you like to learn about air pressure, wind, and water vapor and how they affect weather? Tell how you would find out about this.

_____

_____

_____

_____

_____

**CHAPTER PREVIEW**

Name_____ Date _____

# WEATHER PATTERNS
· · · · · · · · · · · · · · · · · · · · · · · · · · · · · · · · · · · · ·

Pretend that you're a TV weather forecaster preparing your weather map for the evening news show. Draw symbols on the map to show what the weather is like for the day.

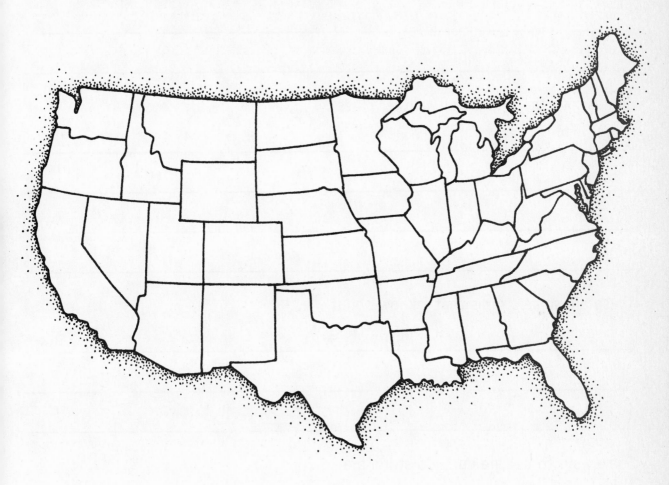

Name_____ Date_____

Dear Journal,

Weather maps give these kinds of information . . .

_____

_____

_____

_____

Clouds give these kinds of weather clues . . .

_____

_____

_____

_____

These are some storms that I know about . . .

_____

_____

_____

Some ways to be safe during a storm are . . .

_____

_____

_____

_____

Name_____ Date_____

# KINDS OF CLOUDS

## Procedure

In the chart below, **write your descriptions** and **draw pictures** of the clouds you observe. **Record** the time of each observation.

| Time | Cloud Description | Cloud Diagram |
|------|-------------------|---------------|
|      |                   |               |

Name_____ Date_____

**List** the categories you used to classify the clouds that you observed.

## Analyze and Conclude

Write the answers to the questions in your book on the lines below.

1. _____

   _____

   _____

2. _____

   _____

   _____

3. _____

   _____

   _____

CHAPTER **3**

Name_____ Date_____

# CLOUDY WEATHER

## Procedure

**Write your predictions** about which types of clouds occur in certain types of weather.

_____

_____

_____

In the chart below, **record your descriptions** of clouds and **record your observations** of weather conditions and temperature.

| Date | Time | Cloud Description | Weather Conditions |
|------|------|-------------------|--------------------|
|      |      |                   |                    |

## Analyze and Conclude

Write the answers to the questions in your book on the lines below.

1. _____

   _____

2. _____

   _____

Name_____ Date_____

 THINK IT WRITE IT

# INVESTIGATION 1
•••••••••••••••••••••••••••••••••••••

**1.** You are going to a picnic and see that the sky is filled with a layer of gray clouds. Should you go to the picnic, or should you stay inside? Explain.

_____

_____

_____

**2.** How can clouds seen from the ground help people predict the weather? What kinds of information do weather satellites provide?

_____

_____

_____

_____

Draw and label a typical cloud from each of the three families of clouds.

**ACTIVITY RECORD**

CHAPTER 3

Name_____ Date_____

# WEATHER MAPS

## Procedure

**Describe** what happened to the high-pressure area over the three-day period shown in weather maps 1, 2, and 3.

_____

_____

_____

**Record** what happened to the low-pressure area over the three-day period.

_____

_____

_____

**Record your observations** of the warm fronts and the cold fronts on the three weather maps.

_____

_____

_____

**Write your prediction** about what weather map 4 will look like.

_____

_____

_____

Name_____ Date_____

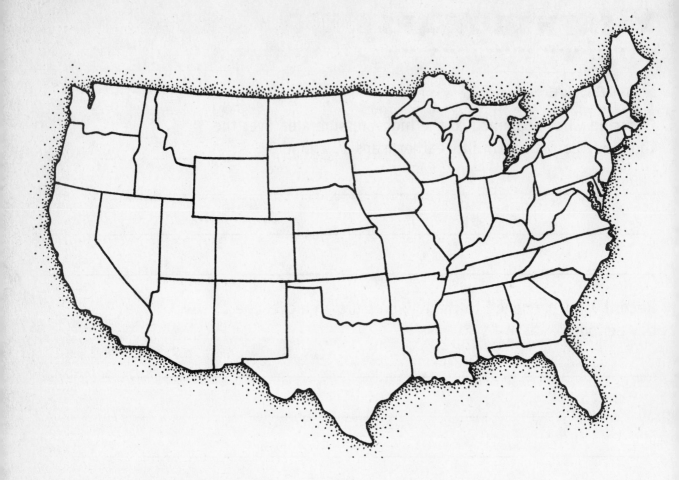

## Analyze and Conclude

Write the answers to the questions in your book on the lines below.

1. _____

_____

_____

2. _____

_____

_____

_____

Name_____ Date_____

# UNIT PROJECT LINK
..............................................

What kinds of changes will you be looking for when you
compare today's weather map with yesterday's weather map?

_____

_____

_____

_____

What changes do you observe in today's weather map com-
pared to yesterday's map?

_____

_____

_____

_____

How could you organize your observations for a week or a
month?

_____

_____

_____

_____

Share this information with your group.

Name_____ Date_____

# PREDICTING THE WEATHER

## Procedure

In the chart below, **record your data** from your weather devices.
**Record your observations** of the types of clouds in the sky and
**record your estimate** of how much of the sky is covered with
clouds.

| Date/Time | Weather Conditions | Measurement or Observations |
|---|---|---|
| | Temperature | |
| | Air pressure | |
| | Wind direction | |
| | Wind speed | |
| | Rain/sleet/snow | |
| | Cloud type | |
| | Cloud cover | |
| | Prediction for tomorrow | |

**Write your prediction** for tomorrow's weather in the chart. Use
the data you collect and weather maps from the newspaper to
help you write your prediction.

**ACTIVITY RECORD**

CHAPTER
3

Name_____ Date_____

## Analyze and Conclude

Write the answers to the questions in your book on the lines below.

1. _____

_____

_____

_____

_____

2. _____

_____

_____

_____

Name_____ Date_____

# UNIT PROJECT LINK

Identify what weather factor each instrument in the weather station measures.

_____

_____

_____

Compare and contrast air pressure, wind speed, cloud type, and cloud cover on fair days and on stormy days.

_____

_____

_____

_____

_____

How many times during the past five days have you made a correct weather prediction?

_____

Have your weather predictions improved over time? Explain.

_____

_____

_____

Share this information with your group.

Name_____ Date_____

# INVESTIGATION 2

**1.** Suppose you are a weather forecaster for your town. What data would you gather to make a prediction about the next day's weather?

_____

_____

_____

**2.** What are four types of information that appear on weather maps?

_____

_____

_____

Draw a diagram of a cold front.

Name_____ Date_____

# STORM SAFETY
• • • • • • • • • • • • • • • • • • • • • • • • • • • •

## Procedure

**List** the types of severe weather that occur in your area. **Record** the safety measures that you should take for each type of severe weather in your area.

**Make a list** of radio and TV stations that you should listen to in case of severe weather.

_____

_____

## Analyze and Conclude

Write the answers to the questions in your book on the lines below.

1. _____

_____

2. _____

_____

Name_____ Date_____

# TORNADO TUBE

## Procedure

**Record your observations** of the water as it drains from the top bottle to the bottom bottle.

_____

_____

_____

## Analyze and Conclude

Write the answers to the questions in your book on the lines below.

1. _____

_____

_____

2. _____

_____

_____

Name_____ Date_____

# INVESTIGATION 3
·······························

**1.** Compare hurricanes and tornadoes. What are some ways in which the two types of storms are similar? What are some ways in which they are different?

_____

_____

_____

_____

_____

**2.** Describe the safety precautions you should take if you are caught outside during a thunderstorm.

_____

_____

_____

Draw a diagram of what a hurricane looks like.

**CHAPTER WRAP-UP**

Name_____ Date _____

# WEATHER PATTERNS
......................................

What can clouds tell you about the weather?

_____

_____

_____

_____

How can maps help you predict weather?

_____

_____

_____

_____

What are some kinds of dangerous weather? How can you stay
safe during such weather?

_____

_____

_____

_____

**CHAPTER WRAP-UP**

Name_____ Date_____

Think about what you learned in Chapter 3 when you answer the following questions.

**1.** What was the most useful thing you learned?

_____

_____

_____

_____

_____

**2.** What surprised you the most as you read this chapter?

_____

_____

_____

_____

_____

**3.** What else would you like to know about forecasting weather? How could you find out about it?

_____

_____

_____

_____

_____

Name_____ Date_____

# SEASONS AND CLIMATE

Think about which of the four seasons is your favorite. Complete the
picture to show what the park looks like during your favorite season.

Name_____ Date_____

Dear Journal,

During my favorite season the weather is . . .

_____

_____

_____

_____

The change of seasons is caused by . . .

_____

_____

_____

_____

I think climate is . . .

_____

_____

_____

_____

**ACTIVITY RECORD**

CHAPTER 4

Name_____ Date_____

# SUNSHINE HOURS

## Procedure

**Write your prediction** about whether the number of sunshine hours is greater in winter or in summer.

_____

In the chart below, **record** the number of sunshine hours for each month.

| Month | Number of Sunshine Hours |
|-------|--------------------------|
| Jan. | _____ |
| Feb. | _____ |
| Mar. | _____ |
| Apr. | _____ |
| May | _____ |
| June | _____ |
| July | _____ |
| Aug. | _____ |
| Sept. | _____ |
| Oct. | _____ |
| Nov. | _____ |
| Dec. | |

Name_____ Date_____

Use the data in your book to **make a graph** below or on a separate sheet of graph paper that shows the number of sunshine hours in a day. Keep your graph in your *Science Notebook*.

## Analyze and Conclude

Write the answers to the questions in your book on the lines below.

1. _____

   _____

2. _____

   _____

3. _____

   _____

Name_____ Date_____

# UNIT PROJECT LINK
· · · · · · · · · · · · · · · · · · · · · · · · · · · · · · · · · · · ·

In which season are you recording data?

_____

Record your daily weather observations in the chart below.

| Date/Time | Temp. (°C) | Precipitation | Air Pressure | Weather Conditions |
|-----------|-----------|---------------|--------------|--------------------|
|           |           |               |              |                    |
|           |           |               |              |                    |
|           |           |               |              |                    |
|           |           |               |              |                    |

How do you think the weather data will change throughout
the different seasons? Explain.

_____

_____

_____

_____

Share this information with your group.

Name_____ Date_____

# INVESTIGATION 1
• • • • • • • • • • • • • • • • • • • • • • • • • • • • • •

**1.** Give two reasons why the Sun heats Earth more in summer than it does in winter.

_____

_____

**2.** Make a drawing to show the positions of the Northern Hemisphere in summer and in winter. Be sure to include the Sun in your picture.

Use a diagram to explain why it's summer in the Northern Hemisphere when it's winter in the Southern Hemisphere.

Name_____ Date_____

# MICROCLIMATES EVERYWHERE!

## Procedure

**Write your prediction** about whether temperature and wind direction will be the same, or different, on each of the sides of your school building.

_____

_____

**Record** in the chart below the air temperature and the wind direction on each side of the school building.

| Building Side | Temperature (°C) | Wind Direction |
|---|---|---|
| | | |

## Analyze and Conclude

Write the answers to the questions in your book on the lines below.

1._____

_____

_____

2._____

_____

Name_____ Date_____

3. _____

_____

_____

4. _____

_____

_____

INVESTIGATE FURTHER!

**EXPERIMENT**

Page E85

**Hypothesize** how the results of this experiment might change over time.

**Predict** whether the same sides of the school building will always be windier or warmer than the other sides.

**Compare** your prediction to your results.

**INVESTIGATE FURTHER**

Name_____ Date_____

**INVESTIGATE FURTHER!**
...........
**RESEARCH**

Page E89

Which city, San Francisco, California, or Wichita, Kansas, is near a large body of water?

**Predict** which city will have a greater change in the average daily temperature from January to June.

**Compare** your prediction with data you have found in an almanac.

**Infer** the effect of being near a large body of water on weather conditions.

Name_____ Date_____

# INVESTIGATION 2

**1.** What are the two main factors that affect the climate of an area? Discuss the three different types of climates.

_____

_____

_____

_____

**2.** Suppose you live near mountains and your friend lives near a large body of water. Describe what type of climate each of you would be likely to have.

_____

_____

_____

_____

Draw tree rings of a young tree that has lived through three years of above average rainfall followed by two years of drought.

**CHAPTER WRAP-UP**

Name_____ Date_____

# SEASONS AND CLIMATE
·····················································

What causes the seasons?

_____

_____

_____

_____

Why are seasons opposite in the Northern Hemisphere and the
Southern Hemisphere?

_____

_____

_____

What factors affect climate?

_____

_____

_____

What are three main types of climate and how do they compare?

_____

_____

_____

_____

Name_____ Date_____

Think about what you learned in Chapter 4 when you answer the following questions.

**1.** What idea was the most difficult for you to understand? What can you do to better understand it?

_____

_____

_____

_____

_____

**2.** What was the most interesting thing you learned?

_____

_____

_____

_____

_____

**3.** What else would you like to learn about the seasons and climate. How would you find out about this?

_____

_____

_____

_____

_____

Name_____ Date_____

# UNIT PROJECT WRAP-UP

Think about the weather forecast you prepared for the Unit Project Big Event. What weather data do you think is the most important for predicting the weather? Explain.

_____

_____

_____

_____

Did you predict the weather accurately in your weather fore-cast? Why is it difficult to accurately predict weather?

_____

_____

_____

_____

_____

What effect do seasons and climate have on weather?

_____

_____

_____

_____

_____

UNIT
F

Name_____ Date_____

# THE BODY'S DELIVERY SYSTEMS

In Unit F you'll investigate the body's delivery systems. For the Unit Project Big Event, you'll produce a quiz show in which contestants are asked questions about these delivery systems. What do you think are the delivery systems in the body? List them below.

_____

_____

_____

What do these body systems deliver?

_____

_____

_____

_____

_____

How can you keep your body systems healthy?

_____

_____

_____

_____

_____

Name_____ Date_____

# UNIT PREVIEW
· · · · · · · · · · · · · · · · · · · · · · · · · · · · · · · · · · · ·

What do you know about the body's delivery systems? What
would you like to learn? List your ideas on the lines below.

_____

_____

_____

_____

_____

_____

_____

_____

_____

_____

**CHAPTER PREVIEW**

Name_____ Date_____

# THE INS AND OUTS OF BREATHING

You are a doctor studying X-rays of a patient's lungs. Draw the lungs on the X-ray film.

Name_____ Date_____

Dear Journal,

These are parts of the respiratory system . . .

_____

_____

_____

When I breathe, these things happen . . .

_____

_____

_____

_____

_____

This happens to the air I breathe in . . .

_____

_____

_____

_____

The air I breathe out has these things in it . . .

_____

_____

_____

Name_____ Date_____

# BREATHE IN AND OUT

## Procedure

**Write your prediction** about how the size of your chest changes as you breathe in and out.

_____

_____

_____

_____

**Record the measurement** of your chest after you breathe in and after you breathe out.

After breathing in: _____

After breathing out: _____

**Calculate** the difference between the two numbers. _____

## Analyze and Conclude

Write the answers to the questions in your book on the lines below.

_____

_____

_____

_____

Name_____ Date_____

# BREATHING RATES

## Procedure

**Record** the number of times you breathe in during one minute while sitting in a chair.

_____

_____

**Write your prediction** about how your breathing rate will change if you sit bent over.

_____

_____

**Record** the number of times you breathe in during one minute while sitting bent over in a chair.

_____

_____

**Write your prediction** about how exercise will affect your breathing rate.

_____

_____

**Record** the number of times you breathe in during one minute after running in place.

_____

_____

**ACTIVITY RECORD**

CHAPTER 1

Name_____ Date_____

## Analyze and Conclude

Write the answers to the questions in your book on the lines below.

1._____

_____

_____

_____

2._____

_____

_____

3._____

_____

_____

Name_____ Date_____

# A BREATHING MACHINE

## Procedure

**Write your prediction** about what will happen to the small balloon when you pull down and push up on the large balloon.

_____

_____

_____

**Record your observations** as you pull down and then push up on the large balloon.

_____

_____

_____

In the space below, **make drawings** of your observations.

**ACTIVITY RECORD**

Name_____ Date_____

## Analyze and Conclude

Write the answers to the questions in your book on the lines below.

1. _____

   _____

   _____

2. _____

   _____

   _____

Name_____ Date_____

# INVESTIGATION 1

**1.** Describe how air is forced into and out of your lungs as you inhale and exhale. Explain the role of the diaphragm in this process.

_____

_____

_____

_____

**2.** In women, the larynx is usually smaller and the vocal cords are shorter than in men. Explain how this affects the sounds of women's voices and of men's voices.

_____

_____

_____

Complete the diagram showing the relationships between the body parts that you use for breathing and those that you use for making sounds.

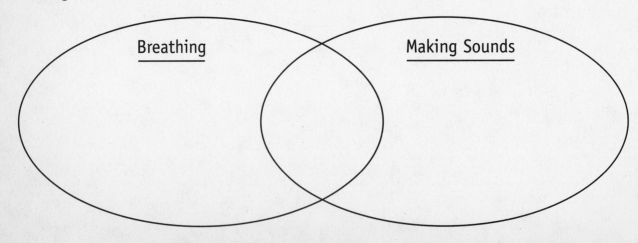

Breathing          Making Sounds

**ACTIVITY RECORD**

CHAPTER 1

Name_____ Date_____

# TAKE A DEEP BREATH

## Procedure

In the chart below, **write your prediction** for the amount of air
you will exhale with a normal breath. Then **record** the actual volume of air you exhale with a normal breath. **Write your prediction**
for the amount of air you will exhale with a deep breath. Then
**record** the actual volume of air you exhale with a deep breath.

| Breath | Air Volume | |
|---|---|---|
| | Predicted Volume | Actual Volume |
| Normal Breath | | |
| Deep Breath | | |

## Analyze and Conclude

Write the answers to the questions in your book on the lines below.

1. _____

_____

_____

2. _____

_____

3. _____

_____

Name_____ Date_____

**Predict** how exercise will affect the amount of air you exhale.

INVESTIGATE FURTHER!
EXPERIMENT
Page F15

**Record the volume** of air you exhale with a single breath after exercising.

**Compare** the volume of one breath at rest with the volume of one breath after exercising.

Why does your nose run?

INVESTIGATE FURTHER!
RESEARCH
Page F17

What causes a sneeze?

Name_____ Date_____

# UNIT PROJECT LINK
· · · · · · · · · · · · · · · · · · · · · · · · · · · · · · · · ·

Write some challenging quiz questions about the parts of the
respiratory system and how the respiratory system works.
Write the answers too.

_____

_____

_____

_____

_____

**Record** the names of the sources that you used to find out
more about the respiratory system.

_____

_____

Write some true-false or multiple-choice questions about the
respiratory system based on the information you found in your
sources. Remember to also write the answers to the questions.

_____

_____

_____

_____

Share this information with your group.

Name_____ Date_____

# INVESTIGATION 2
·············································

**1.** When people get sick with pneumonia, liquids build up in their air sacs. Based on what you've learned, how can pneumonia affect respiration?

_____

_____

_____

**2.** What happens during respiration? How do body cells get oxygen? How do wastes from body cells get to the lungs?

_____

_____

_____

_____

_____

Draw a diagram to show how the lungs absorb oxygen from a breath.

**CHAPTER WRAP-UP**

Name_____ Date_____

# THE INS AND OUTS OF BREATHING
....................................................................

What happens when you breathe in and breathe out?

_____

_____

_____

_____

_____

_____

How does the respiratory system work?

_____

_____

_____

_____

_____

_____

Explain the importance of the air sacs in the lungs.

_____

_____

_____

Name_____ Date_____

Think about what you learned in Chapter 1 when you answer the
following questions.

**1.** What surprised you the most about the workings of the respiratory system?

_____

_____

_____

_____

**2.** What did you learn about the respiratory system that helped
explain something about your body that you've always wondered about?

_____

_____

_____

_____

**3.** What else would you like to know about the respiratory system
and how it works? Explain how you would find out about this.

_____

_____

_____

_____

_____

Name_____ Date_____

# MOVING AND REMOVING MATERIALS

Think about what your heart looks like and how it moves the blood throughout the body. Draw the structure of the heart and the body's circulatory system.

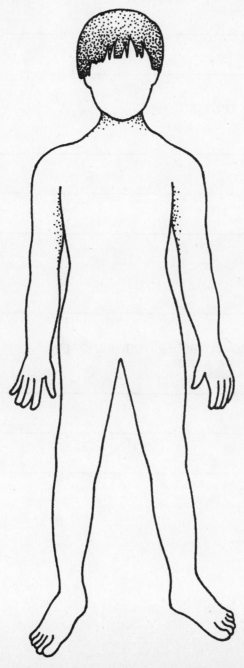

Name_____ Date_____

Dear Journal,

Blood moves through my body like this . . .

_____

_____

_____

_____

_____

Blood is made up of these things . . .

_____

_____

_____

My blood type is . . .

_____

These body parts help remove wastes from my body . . .

_____

_____

_____

CHAPTER 2

Name_____ Date_____

# PUMP ON!
. . . . . . . . . . . . . . . . . . . . .

## Procedure

**Write your prediction** for the number of times you can squeeze a ball in one minute.

_____

_____

**Record** the number of times you can squeeze a ball in one minute.

_____

**Record** how long you can squeeze the ball at a rate of 70 times per minute.

_____

## Analyze and Conclude

Write the answers to the questions in your book on the lines below.

**1.** _____

_____

**2.** _____

_____

_____

Name_____ Date_____

# PULSE POINT
·····························

## Procedure

**Record** your heartbeat rate for one minute at rest.

_____

_____

**Write your prediction** for how your heartbeat rate will change after exercise. **Record** what you think your heartbeat rate per minute will be after exercising.

_____

_____

**Record** your heartbeat rate for one minute after exercising.

_____

## Analyze and Conclude

Write the answers to the questions in your book on the lines below.

**1.** _____

_____

**2.** _____

_____

_____

**3.** _____

_____

Name_____ Date_____

INVESTIGATE
FURTHER!
· · · · · · · · · · ·
RESEARCH

Page F29

How does exercise improve the respiratory and circulatory systems?

If you decided to follow the exercise plan in the book, how would you track your progress?

If you choose to follow the exercise program in the book, record your results below.

Name_____ Date_____

# UNIT PROJECT LINK
......................................................

Write true-false or multiple-choice questions about the parts
of circulatory system and how this system works. Write the
answers too.

_____

_____

_____

_____

_____

_____

_____

Write some quiz questions about the excretory system and
how it works. Remember to also write the answers.

_____

_____

_____

_____

_____

_____

_____

_____

Share this information with your group.

**INVESTIGATION CLOSE**

Name_____ Date_____

# INVESTIGATION 1

· · · · · · · · · · · · · · · · · · · · · · · · · · · · · · · · · · · ·

**1.** How does the heart rate change during and after exercise? Why is this change helpful?

_____

_____

_____

**2.** What are the parts of the circulatory system? Describe how they work together to cause blood to circulate throughout the body.

_____

_____

_____

_____

Draw a diagram showing the path of blood through the heart.

**ACTIVITY RECORD**

Name _____ Date _____

# SKIN SCAN
. . . . . . . . . . . . . . . . . . . . . .

## Procedure

**Record** the features you observe on the skin of your arms and hands. You may do this by **making drawings** of all the features you observe.

**Make a list** of the things that the skin does for the body. Give reasons for each item on your list.

_____

_____

_____

_____

_____

_____

## ACTIVITY RECORD

**CHAPTER 2**

Name_____ Date_____

## Analyze and Conclude

Write the answers to the questions in your book on the lines below.

1. _____

   _____

   _____

   _____

2. _____

   _____

   _____

Name_____ Date_____

# DRINK UP!
• • • • • • • • • • • • • • • • • • • • • • • • •

## Procedure

**Write your prediction** for the amount of liquid that you'll drink in one day.

_____

In the chart below, **record** the amounts and types of liquids you take in during one day. Also **record** the time at which you take in the liquid.

## DRINKS IN A DAY

| Time | Type of Liquid | mL of Liquid |
|------|----------------|--------------|
|      |                |              |

**ACTIVITY RECORD**

Name_____ Date_____

## Analyze and Conclude

Write the answers to the questions in your book on the lines below.

**1.** _____

Calculate your answers here.

**2.** _____

_____

_____

_____

_____

Name_____ Date_____

# INVESTIGATION 2
··············································

**1.** When people have a fever, doctors urge them to drink lots of
liquids. Based on what you know about water balance, infer
why doctors give this advice.

_____

_____

_____

**2.** What are the major body parts of the excretory system?
Describe how they work to get rid of wastes.

_____

_____

_____

_____

Draw a diagram that shows how the skin removes wastes from the
body.

Name_____ Date_____

# MOVING AND REMOVING MATERIALS
••••••••••••••••••••••••••••••••••••••••••••••••••

How does blood flow through your body?

_____

_____

_____

_____

How does your body get rid of wastes?

_____

_____

_____

_____

What role does the circulatory system play in the removal of
wastes from the body?

_____

_____

_____

Use with page F45.

Name_____ Date_____

Think about what you learned in Chapter 2 when you answer the following questions.

**1.** Describe the most interesting thing you learned about the circulatory or excretory system.

_____

_____

_____

_____

**2.** What was the most difficult idea for you to understand about these body systems? Explain how you could help yourself understand the idea better.

_____

_____

_____

_____

**3.** What else would you like to learn about the circulatory and excretory systems? How could you find out about this?

_____

_____

_____

_____

Name_____ Date_____

# KEEPING YOUR SYSTEMS HEALTHY

Add things to this room that you could use to keep your body healthy.

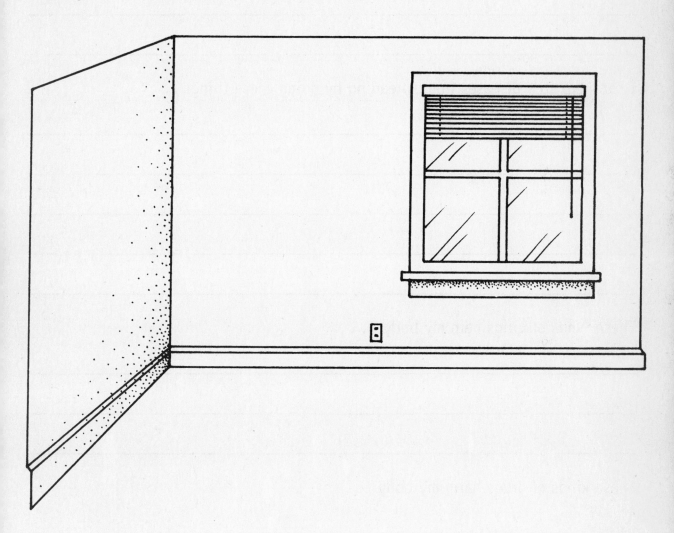

Name_____ Date_____

Dear Journal,

Diseases are caused by . . .

_____

_____

_____

I can help stop diseases from spreading by doing these things . . .

_____

_____

_____

_____

_____

These kinds of drugs help my body . . .

_____

_____

_____

These kinds of drugs harm my body . . .

_____

_____

_____

Name_____ Date_____

# PASS IT ON

## Procedure

**Make a diagram** in the space below that shows how the cold passes through the class. **Record** each student's name as that person gets the cold.

Name_____ Date_____

## Analyze and Conclude

Write the answers to the questions in your book on the lines below.

1. _____

_____

_____

2. _____

_____

_____

3. _____

_____

_____

INVESTIGATE FURTHER!
· · · · · · · · · · · · · · · ·
TAKE ACTION

Page F53

**List** some things an infected person can do to keep from spreading their illness to others.

Which idea on your list will you use for your poster? Explain your choice.

**INVESTIGATE FURTHER**

Name_____ Date_____

**List** some first-aid techniques that you have learned about.

Explain how first-aid techniques help prevent disease.

Describe what your poster about the importance of first aid in helping to prevent disease will look like.

Name_____ Date_____

# INVESTIGATION 1
• • • • • • • • • • • • • • • • • • • • • • • •

**1.** Suppose a family member has a cold. What are some things
you can do to keep from getting the cold?

_____

_____

_____

_____

**2.** What causes disease? What are some ways diseases are
spread?

_____

_____

_____

_____

Complete the table to summarize the different ways in which the
body is defended against disease.

| Body Defenses | |
| --- | --- |
| Keep germs out of the body | Kill germs that have entered the body |
| | |

**ACTIVITY RECORD**

CHAPTER 3

Name_____ Date_____

# AD ADVICE
..........................

## Procedure

**Record** the ads you find that show products containing drugs. Tell whether each ad tries to get people to do healthful or unhealthful things. Explain your decisions.

_____

_____

_____

_____

**List** the ways in which the ads try to get people to use products that might be unhealthful.

_____

_____

_____

**List your ideas** for the ad you'll create.

_____

_____

_____

## Analyze and Conclude

Write the answers to the questions in your book on the lines below.

1. _____

Name_____ Date_____

**2.** _____

_____

_____

_____

**3.** _____

_____

_____

_____

_____

**INVESTIGATE FURTHER!**
·················
**RESEARCH**

Page F59

**List** the names of the children, teen, and adult magazines you looked at. For each magazine record the number of ads that try to get people to do unhealthy things.

Which magazines have the most ads that try to get people to do unhealthful things? Which have the least?

UNIT F

Name_____ Date_____

# UNIT PROJECT LINK

Write some true-false or multiple-choice questions about the immune system and how the body protects itself from disease. Also include the answers to the questions.

_____

_____

_____

_____

_____

_____

Write quiz questions for each of the drugs discussed in the chapter. Remember to also write the answers.

_____

_____

_____

_____

_____

_____

Share this information with your group.

Name_____ Date_____

 # INVESTIGATION 2
··········································

**1.** What are some kinds of helpful drugs? How do they affect the body? What are some kinds of harmful drugs?

_____

_____

_____

_____

_____

_____

**2.** Imagine that some older students are trying to get you to use an illegal drug. How can you make it clear to them that it's something you don't want to do?

_____

_____

_____

_____

When can medicine be harmful to the body?

_____

_____

_____

_____

**CHAPTER WRAP-UP**

Name_____ Date_____

# KEEPING YOUR SYSTEMS HEALTHY

How do diseases spread?

_____

_____

_____

_____

_____

What are harmful and helpful drugs?

_____

_____

_____

_____

_____

Look at the picture you drew on page 297. Explain how it illustrates a way to keep the body healthy.

_____

_____

_____

_____

Name_____ Date_____

Think about what you learned in Chapter 3 when you answer the following questions.

**1.** What surprised you the most as you read this chapter?

_____

_____

_____

**2.** Describe one thing you learned about the importance of taking care of your body.

_____

_____

_____

**3.** What did you learn about keeping your body systems healthy that will help you in your life?

_____

_____

_____

**4.** Describe what else you would like to know about the immune system and about helpful and harmful drugs. How could you find out about it?

_____

_____

_____

_____

UNIT F

Name_____ Date_____

# UNIT PROJECT WRAP-UP

Think about the Body Maze Quiz Show that you produced with your group for the Unit Project Big Event. How did it turn out? What would you do differently next time?

_____

_____

_____

_____

Describe the commercial you produced with your group. Which body system did you use? How does your commercial inform people about keeping their bodies healthy?

_____

_____

_____

_____

How did the Body Maze Quiz Show help you learn more about the circulatory, respiratory, excretory, and immune systems?

_____

_____

_____

_____

_____